Also by Nicolaus Mills

ARGUING

IMMIGRATION

The Debate Over the Changing Face of America

Edited by Nicolaus Mills, with essays by
Toni Morrison, Peggy Noonan,
Francis Fukuyama, Robert Kuttner,
Linda Chavez, Nathan Glazer

A TOUCHSTONE BOOK
Published by Simon & Schuster
New York London Toronto
Sydney Tokyo Singapore

大

TOUCHSTONE
Rockefeller Center
1230 Avenue of the Americas
New York, New York 10020

Designed by Deirdre C. Amthor

Manufactured in the United States of America

1   3   5   7   9   10   8   6   4   2

Library of Congress Cataloging-in-Publication Data

Arguing immigration : the debate over the changing face of
America / edited by Nicolaus Mills ; with essays by
Toni Morrison . . . [et al.].
p.   cm.
"A Touchstone book."
1. United States—Emigration and immigration. 2. United
States—Emigration and immigration—Government policy. I.
Mills, Nicolaus. II. Morrison, Toni.
JV6455.5.A74 1994
325.73—dc20   94-21821
CIP
ISBN: 0-671-89558-3

The following selections in this anthology are reproduced
by permission of the authors, their publishers, or their
agents.

"Immigration Politics," by Linda Chavez. Reprinted by
permission of the author from The International Economy, November–December 1993.

"The Closing Door," by Nathan Glazer. Reprinted by permission of the New Republic. © 1993, The New Republic, Inc.

For Angel Moger and Bill Barry

CONTENTS

Introduction: The Era of the Golden Venture

In the predawn dark of June 6, 1993, the *Golden Venture*, a 150-foot rusting freighter, began dropping its passengers into the cold surf off Rockaway Peninsula in Queens. The trip, which had begun four months earlier in Thailand, was not supposed to end this way for the 296 Chinese who had paid up to $35,000 a piece for the promise of safe entry into America.

The *Golden Venture* was scheduled for a May 17 rendezvous with a smaller ship that would ferry its passengers past immigration authorities and slip them into New York harbor. But the smaller ship never arrived, and desperate to bring their long journey to an end, the smugglers masterminding the trip decided their best alternative was to sail the *Golden Venture* as close to shore as possible, then release their passengers.

It was a risky decision under the best of circumstances. In the dark it turned into a disaster when the *Golden Venture* struck a sandbar. Ten of the ship's passengers died trying to make it to shore. Only luck and heroic rescue efforts by the police and Coast Guard saved more from drowning in the fifty-three-degree Atlantic waters.

The Rockaway beach where the *Golden Venture* hit a sandbar was ironically just two hundred yards from Jacob Riis Park. In his 1890 book *How the Other Half Lives,* the Danish-born Riis provided America with a full and detailed account of what life in the slums meant for most poor immigrants, but one hundred years later there was no Jacob Riis waiting to do the same for the passengers of the *Golden Ven-*

ture. Nor was there a massive public outcry to let them stay. In the nation's editorial columns, the story of the *Golden Venture* became instead an occasion for choosing up sides: for arguing about who should and shouldn't be allowed into the country. As the television pictures of the shivering passengers of the *Golden Venture* faded from memory, it also became clear what would have happened if their trip had gone as planned. A nation that has absorbed an estimated five million *illegal* immigrants during the last ten years would have taken in several hundred more, and nobody would have been the wiser.

It was Israel Zangwill, a contemporary of Riis, who in a 1908 play that opened in Washington popularized the idea of America as a melting pot. David Quixano, the hero of Zangwill's play, is a young Russian Jewish composer who falls in love with another immigrant, Vera, the daughter of a Russian army officer. Their American marriage defies the "blood hatreds" of old Europe and reflects David's belief that "America is God's melting pot, where all the races of Europe are melting and reforming." Zangwill's metaphor comes from steelmaking, but the idea of the immigrant who blends in and becomes a new man or woman dates back to a much earlier time. In his 1782 *Letters from an American Farmer* Hector St. John de Crèvecoeur used the idea of melting to answer his own question, "What then is the American, this new man?" With an optimism that like Zangwill's ignored the plight of those who came in chains and those who were here before the first colonists arrived, Crèvecoeur declared, "Here individuals of all nations are melted into a new race of men, whose labours and posterity will one day cause great changes in the world."

In the America of the 1990s, nobody talks about melting pots very much, let alone uses the kind of patriotic language that prompted Theodore Roosevelt to declare, "Either a man is an American and nothing else, or he is not an American at all." When we speak about national unity, our most hopeful figure of speech is usually that of a mosaic, and for many, even a mosaic seems too optimistic. We no longer have the social confidence that as recently as 1984 allowed audiences to delight in a film like *Moscow on the Hudson*, in which Robin Williams, playing a Russian refugee, finds himself sheltered by a black family, aided by a Cuban lawyer, and in love with an Italian immigrant.

Not since the turn of the century has immigration been so controversial. At a time when identity politics, with its emphasis on race and ethnicity, shapes national elections as well as grade school curriculums, few believe that our newest immigrants—over 80 percent are persons of color—are easily going to blend into American society. Still fewer are so secure that they are above fearing that their jobs or their tax rates may not be adversely affected by this latest wave of immigration. In a 1993 *Time*/CNN poll, 73 percent of those questioned favored strict limits on immigration.

In his classic study of immigration, *Send These to Me*, historian John Higham divides America's earlier immigration into two broad periods. What he calls the First Immigration was primarily an eighteenth-century undertaking that lasted until 1803 and brought with it white, predominantly English-speaking, mainly Protestant Europeans. By contrast, the Second Immigration, which began in the 1820s and lasted until the immigration restriction laws of the 1920s, was, Higham notes, a more diverse and controversial phenomenon. It brought more Catholics and Jews, more Southern Europeans and non-English speakers. Behind it lay the breakdown of the traditional agricultural system in Europe and a transportation revolution that made America increasingly accessible.

If we apply Higham's analysis to the present, it makes sense to think of today's newcomers as part of a Third Immigration that began in the late 1960s. What they have done is extend the patterns of the Second Immigration. With their Asian and Hispanic roots, today's immigrants are, relative to America's overall population, more diverse than any previous immigrant wave. They have been aided by another transportation revolution (the cheap plane flight), and they have left their homelands because of social and economic conditions that according to the United Nations are responsible for 19.7 million refugees living outside their borders and another twenty-four million displaced within their own borders.

They are also a group few anticipated would come in such numbers—8.6 million in the 1980s alone, according to U.S. Census figures. As sociologist Nathan Glazer notes, "When one considers our present immigration policies, it seems we have insensibly reverted to mass immigration without ever having made a decision to do so." To complicate matters still further, our immigration debate has not broken down along the usual political lines. These days we might expect liberals to favor relatively open immigration, seeing it in terms of a politics of compassion, and we might expect conservatives, worried about multiculturalism and an expanding welfare state, to want severe restrictions on immigration.

But the opposite is often the case. Liberals are among those with the deepest reservations about immigration. Now, as in the past, trade unionists consistently voice their fears over the way legal and illegal immigrants are used to hold wages down. By contrast, free-market conservatives are some of the strongest advocates of increased immigration. "If Washington still wants to do something about immigration," the *Wall Street Journal* declared in a July Fourth editorial, "we propose a five-word constitutional amendment: There shall be open borders." In his second annual Christmas message, Ronald Reagan was just as outspoken. "I know we're crowded and we have real problems with refugees," he said, "but I honestly hope and pray we can always find room."

What is certain is that in the 1990s our national debate over immigration is sure to increase in intensity. "We must not—we will not—surrender our borders to those who wish to exploit our history of compassion and justice," President Clinton declared in the wake of reports that a suspect in the

World Trade Center bombing of 1993 had fraudulently entered the country by asking for political asylum. But the President's remarks touched on more than just the asylum issue. As he found out after a scandal arose when it was learned that Zoë Baird, his first nominee for attorney general, had hired two illegal Peruvian immigrants to work for her, we cannot discuss immigration these days without also talking about the kind of country we are. The future of immigration in America is inseparable from our sense of how closely we want to live together, how many jobs our economy can support, how diverse we want our society to be.

· · · ·

The decision that paved the way for the massive immigration we are now experiencing goes back to the immigration reforms of 1965. For the preceding forty-one years, immigration to America had been reduced dramatically by the Johnson-Reed Act of 1924. Passed at a time when anti-immigration feeling was running high, the Immigration Act of 1924 set a yearly limit of 150,000 on immigrants from outside the Western Hemisphere and then divided the 150,000 into quotas based on a country's share of the total population in 1920. The national origins system favored the descendants of those who had been here the longest—the British and Northern Europeans.

When a *Los Angeles Times* headline hailed the new law as a "Nordic Victory," it was not mistaken. Chinese, as a result of extensions of the Chinese Exclusion Act of 1882 (it would not be repealed until 1943), were already barred, and Japanese, as a result of a provision in the 1924 act excluding immigrants who were ineligible to become citizens, were also effectively kept out. The immigration tide that from 1880 to 1920 had brought 23.5 million people to America was over. From 1921 to 1930 immigration dropped to just over four million. In the Depression years of the 1930s, it was barely half a million, and in the 1940s, despite special legislation that in 1948 paved the way for hundreds of thousands of displaced persons to come to America, immigration only reached a million.

The McCarran-Walter Immigration and Nationality Act of 1952 did little to change this pattern. Passed over the veto of President Harry Truman, who wanted a more liberal immigration law, the McCarran-Walter Act eliminated racial barriers to naturalization and thereby to immigration. The act still, however, retained most of the quota preferences of the 1924 law. Asians could now enter America as immigrants, but their numbers, like those of Southern Europeans, were kept low. From 1951 to 1960 only 2.5 million immigrants came to the United States.

The Immigration and Nationality Act Amendments of 1965 undid this pattern. Passed in the middle of the civil rights revolution, the 1965 law reflected the optimism of the Great Society and the views of a coalition of Jews, Catholics, and liberals who for years had fought against the biases of the 1924 law. The new amendments put a limit on immigration from the Western Hemisphere for the first time. Of the 290,000 immigrants who came under the law's quota restrictions, only 120,000 could be from the Western Hemisphere. But in every other respect the 1965 amendments were revolutionary. The new bill abandoned all efforts to distinguish among immigrants on the basis of their race or their historical link to America. Up to 20,000 people could come from any single nation. The dominating principle was now family reunification. Eighty percent of the numerically limited visas were for close relatives of American citizens or residents.

The coalition behind the act saw it, as President Johnson declared at the Statue of Liberty signing ceremony, as a law that "repairs a deep and painful flaw in American justice." But the act's proponents did not believe it would substantially change immigration numbers. "Our cities will not be flooded with a million immigrants annually," Senator Edward Kennedy, one of the act's sponsors, declared. "Under the proposed bill the present level of immigration remains substantially the same." His brother Robert Kennedy, while attorney general, was equally optimistic, assuring a House subcommittee that the number of immigrants "to be expected from the Asia-Pacific triangle would be approximately five thousand."

What neither the President nor the Kennedys foresaw, however, was that the 1965 law contained a major loophole as a result of its family reunification policy, which allowed the parents, spouses, and minor children of any adult American citizen to enter the country *without* being subject to numerical restrictions. As Asian and Latin immigrants with large extended families replaced European immigrants, the immigration multiplier—the number of admittances attributable to one immigrant—began to change dramatically. The fifth preference of the new law, one that placed brothers and sisters high on the quota list, accelerated the process still more. Between 1971 and 1980, 4.5 million immigrants were admitted to the United States. Then in the 1980s the numbers climbed to a peak they had not reached since the turn of the century. By the end of the decade, our current annual pattern of a million or more refugees, most of them in flight from the poverty and violence of the Third World, became the norm.

The result has been a national backlash against immigration. We like the idea of a restored Ellis Island because we can sentimentalize the nineteenth-century immigration struggle it represents. But increasingly we are at home with the distinction between past and present immigration that former Colorado governor Richard Lamm, author of *The Immigration Time Bomb,* recently drew when he noted, "Immigration has been good for America, but the public policy of immigration was made when we were an empty continent and could absorb unlimited amounts of unskilled labor." In a 1993 *Newsweek* poll 59 percent of those asked said past immigration was good for the country, but only 29 percent said that was true today. Sixty percent replied that immigration was now harmful.

Despite this backlash, since the 1980s legislative efforts to deal with immigration have only added to the number of immigrants America takes in each year. The 1986 Immigration Reform and Control Act (IRCA) is a classic case of a law that has done just that. Passed after years of wrangling over the best way to halt illegal immigration, IRCA was designed to mix compassion for illegal immigrants with job protection for American citizens. Any illegal immigrant who entered the United States before 1982 and lived here continuously since then was granted amnesty. In turn employers who hired illegal aliens were now subject to fines and, if a pattern of hiring illegals could be found, jail sentences as well. IRCA offered amnesty to an estimated 3.7 illegal immigrants (2.6 million accepted amnesty), and for the first two years, there was a drop in the number of illegal immigrants entering America. But it soon became clear that the employer sanctions of IRCA had no teeth and that its safeguards were easily avoided (in one recent case netting a consulting firm $5.7 million for helping process 5,600 false amnesty applications). By the late 1980s illegal immigration began to rise again. The chairman of the U.S. Commission on Immigration Reform acknowledges that as many as 500,000 illegals now enter the country each year.

Increased immigration has also resulted from the most recent immigration reform, the Immigration Act of 1990. Designed to overcome the 1965 law's emphasis on family reunification, the 1990 law was drafted with the idea of supplying skilled workers and needed capital (there are 10,000 visas for those willing to invest $1 million in a new business that employs at least ten workers). But the congressional coalition responsible for passage of the law refused to make its implementation dependent on a corresponding reduction in the number of immigrants admitted on the basis of family relationships. The 1990 law thus does nothing to reduce the flow of immigrants to America. It only raises to 140,000 the number of immigrants who can be admitted on the basis of their job skills or the special contributions they offer. As labor economist Vernon M. Briggs, Jr., points out in his *Mass Immigration and the National Interest*, "The Immigration Act of 1990 is essentially an expansion in scale of the previously existing immigration system that had been in effect since 1965. Its most important characteristic is that it increases legal immigration levels by about 35 percent over the previously authorized levels."

Changes in American refugee law have complicated matters still further. Prior to 1980, the United States defined a refugee as someone fleeing a Communist country, a Communist-dominated area, or the Middle East. The Refugee Act of 1980 changed our Cold War bias. In accord with the United Nations Protocol on Refugees, a refugee was now defined as someone unable or unwilling to return to his country because of a "well-founded fear of persecution on account of race, religion, nationality, membership in a particular social group, or political opinion." The result, as with the liberal reforms of the 1965 law, has been an increase in the number of people admitted into the country. In 1975 there were just two hundred asylum applications. By 1992 asylum applications were up to 103,000 per year and the backlog was over 300,000. Since the law entitles asylum claimants who make it to America to remain in the country until they have a hearing, the likelihood is that the backlog will continue to grow (the United States has only 150 asylum officers) along with the pressure to admit anyone who declares he or she is fleeing oppression.

• • •

In happier times the prospect of taking in a million or more immigrants per year might not cause such a public outcry. The current influx of immigrants is much lower than the 1900–20 peak when considered as a percentage of our population. Immigrants were 1 percent of our population then. They are approximately one-third of 1 percent now. Even the percentage of foreign-born living in America is not what it used to be. It 1910 it was 13.5 percent. In 1940 it was 8.8 percent. Today it is 7.9 percent—a considerable leap from 1980 when it was 6.2 percent but still well below levels we have previously absorbed. In the present circumstances there is, however, no way statistical analysis is going to dampen the nation's immigration fears.

At their most extreme these fears are epitomized by a highway sign in Southern California. Caution, the sign warns: in black silhouette against a yellow background it shows a family running. It is the West Coast equivalent of a New England deer-crossing sign, but posted as it is, along a highway where illegals enter the country from Mexico, the sign carries a very different message. Here, it says, are people so intent on flight that they are vulnerable to traffic. Here is a problem so beyond control that all the government can do is issue warnings.

Even, however, when the immigration debate is not colored by exaggerated fears, the passions it evokes run deep. So much is at stake, and so often the debate is based on generalities that treat immigrants as a single entity rather than groups that bring with them different educational and work qualifications. Nowhere are these passions more evident than in the debate over the costs and benefits of immigration. At the heart of that debate is the question of jobs—does immigration improve our labor supply or merely displace native-born workers struggling to stay in the labor force?

In 1863, in the midst of the Civil War, Abraham Lincoln confidently asked Congress to establish "a system for the encouragement of immigration." There was, Lincoln noted, "still a great deficiency in every field of industry, especially in agriculture and our mines, as well as of iron and coal." Over 130 years later, with blue-collar factory jobs at a minimum (more than three million have been lost since 1979) and white-collar firms like IBM and Eastman Kodak rapidly downsizing, the labor needs Lincoln called on Congress to remedy no longer exist. The economic debate over who to let in and who to keep out takes place in a country that sees opportunities contracting, not expanding.

The pro-immigration side of the costs-and-benefits debate is bolstered by analyses that show immigrants reviving dying neighborhoods and taking low-paying jobs that native-born workers refuse. Without immigrants our remaining garment industry would have already gone overseas and our hotel and restaurant business would be greatly reduced, pro-immigrationists contend. They point to studies that show per-capita income among immigrants is actually higher than that of native-born Americans and that for every one-hundred-person increase in the population of adult immigrants the number of new jobs rose by forty-six. By contrast, for every one hundred new native-born Americans the number of jobs rose by only twenty-five.

Immigration restrictionists, on the other hand, see a different picture. They look at California, where manufacturing has grown five times the national average in recent years while wages have grown 12 percent more slowly in the state and 15 percent more slowly in Los Angeles. Immigration, they argue, accounts for this disparity as well as for the kind of economic downturn that has transformed drywall construction in California from high-paying union work to low-paying nonunion work. Common sense, immigration restrictionists insist, tells us that in an economy that already has high levels of unemployment the arrival of new workers, eager for almost any job, can only harm those trying to hold on.

The welfare side of the costs-and-benefits debate produces similarly sharp divisions. Pro-immigrationists point to studies showing that immigrants pay more in taxes ($85 billion) than they take out of the welfare system ($24 billion) and conclude that immigration is a plus. Restrictionists counter with another set of figures. They contend that immigration advocates don't take into account the cost of job displacement, and they argue that it is insufficient to balance the taxes immigrants pay against the welfare they receive. A more accurate measure must be based on a broad range of public programs, from parks to schools, benefiting immigrants—and in these terms immigrants are a $16 billion yearly drain on the economy. Even more alarming, restrictionists contend, are other recent trends. By comparison with immigrants of twenty years ago, those arriving today are significantly less skilled. In 1990 over 9 percent of immigrant households received public assistance as compared to 7 percent of native households, and the welfare payment the immigrant household received was also high—$1,400 more than for the typical native household.

When the debate over immigration shifts from costs and benefits to race, it takes on a different tone. Nobody on either side wants to be accused of racism or nativism. The immigration tide of the last fifteen years suggests that our population growth is increasingly supplying the numbers that would make formidable the kind of Rainbow Coalition Jesse Jackson wants to bring about. In the 1980s, according to the census, the Asian population in America rose by 107 percent and the Hispanic population increased by 53 percent.

The problem is that this increase in new minorities has often made life harder for older minorities. It has not been easy for minorities to act in concert or to find common ground, as the struggles of Latinos, Asians, and blacks for representation on the Los Angeles City Council shows. New immigrants have frequently acquired their power at the expense of native-born minorities. More important, without intending to, new immigrants have thown into question the old arguments for affirmative action. In his 1965 Howard University speech that became the basis for affirmative action, Lyndon Johnson argued, "You do not take a person who, for years, has been hobbled by chains and liberate him, bring him to the starting line and then say, 'You are free to compete with all others' and still justly believe you have been completely fair." Johnson's point was that America's racial history made it necessary to compensate blacks for damage done over centuries. But that causal link is undermined, when, as is now the case, a new minority immigrant is as eligible for affirmative action as a fifteenth-generation African American. Not only are the two in competition with each other for the same affirmative-action slots, but making the minority immigrant an affirmative-action beneficiary subverts the historic rationale for affirmative action. It no longer becomes a remedy for past wrongs but a system of proportional representation.

The cultural arguments over immigration also have their roots in race, but the engine that drives them is the issue of diversity and the fear that American culture is fragmenting beyond repair. All too often the fragmentation fear ignores what Nathan Glazer and Daniel Patrick Moynihan showed three decades ago in their classic study *Beyond the Melting Pot*: namely, immigrants and their children held on to the culture they left behind as well as adapted to the culture they found in America. Nonetheless, there remain valid reasons for worrying that the new immigration may increase the cultural schisms already dividing America. Nowadays in colleges it is routine for the administration to make sure a course on ethnicity or race is taught by a professor whose ethnicity or race matches the course subject, and in public high schools history is increasingly taught in such a way that identity politics and group pride are the paramount issues for students. Given these trends, immigration restrictionists ask, doesn't immigration accelerate the cultural separatism now under way? Don't today's immigrants have, in fact, more to gain from a cultural perspective that defines America as centerless and emphasizes a politics of difference?

Even asylum, the area in the immigration debate in which goodwill remains the overriding issue, is not immune from questions about those we should take in and those we should exclude. In the first three decades after World War II, it was relatively easy to have a generous asylum policy. The Displaced Persons Act of 1948, which eventually allowed

400,000 refugees to enter the United States, proved relatively uncontroversial, as did our decision to admit Hungar-
ian refugees after that country's failed 1956 revolution and
Cuban refugees after Fidel Castro came to power. But in recent years, faced with a worldwide refugee crisis of epic pro-
portions, we have been having second thoughts about our
asylum policy.

For those who view retreat on asylum as a case of pulling
up the ladder, our recent actions are a betrayal of our own
history. They point to the double standard we have used in
welcoming refugees from Communist regimes and turning
back those from a country like Haiti with a right-wing dic-
tatorship. What, they ask, except racism or outdated ideological fears, can explain our thinking? Why in the 1990s
do we have fewer asylum officers than Germany or tiny
Sweden?

Those who believe we need to limit asylum acknowledge
that American refugee policy has often functioned hypocrit-
ically. They contend, however, that we find ourselves in a position in which as a country that accepts more immigrants
than all other industrial nations *combined* we are in danger
of being overwhelmed by asylum seekers. From Chinese
who want asylum because of their country's birth-control
policies to victims of the civil war in the former Yugoslavia,
there is, the defenders of limited asylum argue, an endless
list of people we might take in. Our procedures for granting
temporary asylum to those who arrive on our shores and
claim they are fleeing political oppression have already
made us vulnerable to terrorists and those whose real goal is
escaping the poverty of the Third World. What we need to
do, the restrictionists conclude, is figure out better ways of
guarding our borders. After all, even Doris Meissner, ap-
pointed by President Clinton as head of the Immigration
and Naturalization Service, admits, "The asylum system is
broken, and we need to fix it."

• • •

A century ago our immigration fears were voiced in much cruder terms. In 1845 at its July Fourth convention, the restrictionist Native American Party did not hesitate to decry "the peril from the rapid and enormous increase of the body of residents of foreign birth, imbued with foreign feelings and of an ignorant and immoral character." As the Civil War drew closer, Senator Garrett Davis of Kentucky warned that the union was threatened not only by the battle over slavery but by "the hordes of Europe" with "their ignorance and their pauperism, mixed up with large amounts of idleness, moral degradation and crime." Even those who should have known better did not hesitate to describe the immigrant as less than human. "He resembles for the time the dog who sniffs around the freshly acquired bone, giving it a push and a lick," Henry James wrote in *The American Scene* of 1907. "Let not the unwary, therefore, visit Ellis Island," he warned.

Today, those in the public eye are much shrewder about voicing their immigration fears, but immigrant bashing goes on all the same. At its rawest it takes the form of overt violence, as in the attacks on Korean stores during the Los Angeles riots in 1992. But it can also be part of mainstream politics, as Pat Buchanan showed—first at the 1992 Republican National Convention in announcing the time had come to "take back our culture," and later in a *Washington Times* editorial warning that immigration will turn the United States into the Brazil of North America.

In the midst of such immigrant bashing, no end of alternative proposals abound. Liberal columnist Robert Kuttner has suggested a national identity card. Nobel Prize–winning economist Gary Becker has proposed an auction system for selling immigrant visas. Immigration expert Stephen Moore has proposed putting more emphasis on admitting immigrants with needed skills.

None of these plans represents, however, more than a piecemeal approach to our immigration dilemma. "There is a limit to our powers of assimilation, and when it is exceeded, the country suffers from something very much like indigestion," the *New York Times* observed more than a century ago. Once again we need to ask ourselves, what is the limit—emotional and economic—of our powers of coping with immigration?

Confronting that question will not be easy. Candor will mean acknowledging that for many talk about our current immigration problems is simply another way of voicing fears about America becoming a nonwhite nation. But candor will also mean not automatically labeling racist or nativist those who see present immigration patterns as a threat to the precarious cultural and ethnic balance America now maintains.

The common wisdom among most immigration experts is that in the 1990s there will not be a dramatic change in our current immigration policy. As Peter Salins of the Manhattan Institute of Policy Research writes, "Those both for and against immigration behave as if it were politically conceivable that the United States might drastically cut immigration again, as we did in the 1920s, and as if our borders could be effectively sealed if we chose to do so. In spite of resurgent nativism, any proposal to sharply curtail legal immigration would meet massive resistance across the political spectrum—from liberals who see open immigration as a basic ingredient of the universalist American idea to conservatives attached to free markets and open international borders."

Salins may be right, although nearly one hundred members of Congress have signed onto bills that would slash current immigration by at least 65 percent. But whatever decision we make about the future of immigration will carry a high price. In contrast to France, which has officially set zero immigration as a goal, or Germany, which insists it is "not a country of immigrants," we as a nation can only talk about restricting immigration in terms of changing a history that made hopes and values more important than birthplace or ancestry. The actual process of restricting immigration—especially if it means a Border Patrol army, fingerprint identity cards, and tougher asylum laws—may, moreover, come with too high an ethical and financial cost.

On the other hand, continuing our current immigration policies will also impose burdens. We no longer have an unsettled West or young industries in need of raw manpower. We are a country in the midst of economic and cultural change, relying on an elaborate welfare system to support a growing segment of the population. The gap between those who thrive in our high-tech, informational economy and those who can no longer make it widens along with our doubts about who we are collectively. We are even unsure if the history our children study in school or the language we speak in public is truly shared.

The real question is not whether in the 1990s we can avoid making painful choices about immigration. It is whether we can make those choices through debate that, as much as humanly possible, resists appeals to old stereotypes and new hatreds.

I. To Open or Close the Door

Immigration Politics
Linda Chavez

Linda Chavez is director of the Center for the New American Community in Washington, D.C., and the former executive director of the U.S. Commission on Civil Rights. She is the author of *Out of the Barrio: Toward a New Politics of Hispanic Assimilation.* "Immigration Politics" was first published in *The International Economy,* November–December 1993.

THE UNITED STATES has always taken pride in its immigrant heritage. But with an estimated 1.3 million new entrants arriving each year, the American welcome mat may soon wear thin. The social contract traditionally kept between the host and immigrant populations has been radically transformed. Both legal and illegal immigrants have regained entitlement over the last two decades to a wide array of welfare programs unavailable to previous generations. Public support for immigration has subsequently eroded since 1965, when the United States liberalized its immigration laws. Only 33 percent of the country wanted fewer immigrants that year, but disfavor grew to 42 percent in 1977, 49 percent in 1986, and hit 65 percent in 1993. A *Newsweek* cover story reported that 60 percent of Americans believe that immigration is a "bad thing" for the country today. Even immigrant populations are souring on immigration—according to the 1993 Latino National Political Survey, 65 percent of Hispanics feel that immigration has spiraled out of control.

31

Nobody tracks poll numbers more closely than politicians. In Congress and many state legislatures, lawmakers of all political stripes are rushing to introduce bills restricting both legal and illegal immigration. Calls to slow immigration to the United States have not yet reached the frantic European pitch, but the issue surely threatens to become a hot-button political issue in the next few years. President Clinton has promised to beef up border security, reversing an earlier budget proposal that actually would have cut ninety-three agents from the Border Patrol. He also used illegal immigration as a selling point for the North American Free Trade Agreement, correctly arguing that its passage would eventually reduce the number of unlawful aliens.

California governor Pete Wilson also jumped on the immigration bandwagon in 1993, commanding national headlines in August when he proposed a set of sweeping new laws to deter illegal immigration. Under his plan, Wilson would refuse citizenship to children born on U.S. soil to illegal immigrants, end the legal requirement that states pay for emergency medical care of illegal immigrants, deny public education to the children of illegal immigrants, and manufacture a national identification card. Many considered his suggestions outlandish—their complete implementation would probably require passing a new constitutional amendment, overturning a Supreme Court ruling, and writing several controversial laws from scratch. Nevertheless, Wilson's sagging approval ratings actually bounced upward for the first time in many months.

Immigrants currently make up about 8 percent of the U.S. population, which is only about half of what it was during the peak immigration years at the turn of the century. Nonetheless, the impact of immigrants is uneven and enormous. Immigrants tend to live near other immigrants, so a handful of cities and communities are home to most of the country's immigrants. Last year alone, more than a quarter million legal immigrants settled in California, a 23 percent increase from the previous year. Of these immigrants, some

90,000 moved to Los Angeles County. Although 54 percent of California's immigrants hail from Asia, nearly 47,000 Mexicans accounted for the greatest number of immigrants from any one country. Most of these Mexicans did not travel far, settling in the southern end of the state.

Precise numbers on illegal immigrants are hard to come by for obvious reasons, though reliable estimates put the national figure at about 300,000 per year. More than any other place, they choose to reside in California. Californians until recently seemed resigned if not happy to accept their new neighbors, but no longer. New polls show that 86 percent of Californians consider illegal immigration a problem, and nearly three-quarters of them want the National Guard to patrol the southern border to keep out illegal aliens. Some politicians have gone so far as to suggest building a wall or fence enclosing the region. This change in attitude springs mainly from two sources: a stagnant local economy and the proliferation of immigrant entitlements.

The 1991 recession, military base closings, and cutbacks in defense spending have had especially harmful consequences for the California economy. State unemployment levels are higher than the national average. Last year's $3.4 billion state budget shortfall only made matters worse. Immigrants have traditionally been a source of the state's economic growth, helping keep afloat certain domestic industries—such as clothing and auto parts manufacturing—by providing a low-wage source of labor. Studies in the 1980s estimated that both legal and illegal immigrants were net contributors to the California economy, paying more in taxes than they received in services and creating jobs rather than displacing American workers. But the withering job market has made immigrants an easy target of anxiety, especially as out-of-work immigrants join other unemployed Californians in seeking public assistance. Today, the debate is not only about whether immigrants compete with native-born Americans for jobs, but what they cost taxpayers in welfare and other public assistance payments. The question has become particularly explosive with respect to illegal aliens.

Although illegal aliens are technically ineligible for welfare payments in California and elsewhere in the United States, many obtain benefits using forged documents. Virtually all are eligible for expensive forms of public assistance, such as emergency medical treatment and public education for their children. Many illegal immigrants actually cross the border simply to give birth within the United States, an act that automatically confers citizenship upon the child. For many of these parents, payments in the form of Aid to Families with Dependent Children await them. The United States, of course, has an interest in providing services like police and fire protection to illegal aliens and their communities, but even these modest offerings take a toll on the public trust. Many American resent the fact that illegal immigrants live in the country at all. Meanwhile, some immigrant advocates argue that the government should provide much wider benefits than it currently does, since many illegal immigrants will eventually become legal residents and naturalized citizens. By taking care of their educational and health requirements early on, the argument goes, we keep them from falling into a permanent second-class status that will sap resources later.

Immigrant-related stresses in the school systems have both economic and cultural ramifications. In Los Angeles, for instance, 160,000 non–English-speaking students receive instruction not only in Spanish, but also Armenian, Korean, Cantonese, Tagalog, Russian, and Japanese. School administrators almost uniformly insist on teaching Hispanic immigrant children in Spanish rather than immediately immersing them in special English classes. In these settings, multiculturalism quickly becomes divisive as children who desperately need to learn English are shuffled into classes that offer only native-language instruction. Ironically, many of the most disadvantaged recent Mexican immigrants are Mayans or Mexican Indians who do not speak Spanish.

Nevertheless, California cannot find as many certified Spanish-speaking teachers as it would like; it recently accepted twenty bilingual teachers and 40,000 Spanish-language textbooks from the government of Mexico. Perhaps California will succeed where Mexico has failed for half a millennium and turn these Mayans into Spanish speakers. That accomplishment would certainly have some advantages for those who return to Mexico, but it will not help those remaining in the United States.

Despite all of these problems, immigrants remain a tremendous national asset. They have helped revitalize many urban neighborhoods and maintain a tax base in cities like New York and Los Angeles. Per-capita income among immigrants is higher than that of native-born Americans, $15,003 compared with $14,367. The figure is highest among Africans, at $20,177. Immigrants are also slightly more likely to work in the labor force than the native-born. Some groups far outpace U.S. workers, including Haitians, Jamaicans, Salvadorans, Guatemalans, Peruvians, and Filipinos. Among each of these groups, labor force participation rates are at least ten points higher than those of the native-born. A drastic reduction in immigration would likely have a negative impact through labor shortages and driving up wages.

The immigrant landscape today is very different than it was at the turn of the century. Yesteryear's "huddled masses, yearning to breathe free" were not thrust into the bosom of the welfare state. Advocacy groups did not demand immigrant entitlements that increase public cost and private resentment. We must curb both the abuses and anomalies of the current system, particularly to discourage dependency and to stop isolating immigrant children in linguistic ghettos. Although the immigration restrictionists appear to be winning over the public, they will not be as successful in stemming the tide of immigration. The last effort to do so—the Immigration Reform and Control Act of 1986—succeeded only in penalizing employers like Zoë Baird while having no discernible impact on reducing illegal immigration. The wiser course—and one with broader economic benefits—will be to examine the entitlement programs that drain resources and entrap immigrant and native-born generations alike.

The Closing Door
Nathan Glazer

Nathan Glazer is coeditor of *The Public Interest*. His books include *Ethnic Dilemmas, Affirmative Discrimination,* and, with Daniel Moynihan, *Beyond the Melting Pot.* "The Closing Door" first appeared in the *New Republic,* December 27, 1993.

CLEARLY WE ARE at the beginning of a major debate on immigration. The issue has been raised most immediately in recent months by the immigrants, legal and illegal, now charged with the devastating bombing of the World Trade Center and with planning the bombing of other major New York buildings and New York transportation links;* and by the interception of vessels carrying illegal Chinese immigrants approaching New York and California. But the issue is larger than how to control illegal immigration, difficult as this is. Despite the presence of a mass of laws, regulations, and court rulings controlling immigration, we are shaky as a polity on the largest questions that have to be answered in determining an immigration policy: what numbers should we admit, of what nations and races, on what basis should we make these decisions, and how should we enforce them?

To answer these questions we will have to define our expectations about immigration, its effects on American soci-

---

*Since this article was written, a jury has convicted the men charged with bombing the World Trade Center.

ety, economy, polity. It is a serious question whether the American political system is capable of giving any coherent response to these questions. Indeed, it could be argued that we have not been capable of a coherent response since the key decisions, now execrated in all quarters, of the 1920s.

I should say execrated in almost all quarters, for there are now bold voices, such as Thomas Fleming in the obscure journal *Chronicles* and Peter Brimelow in the not-at-all-obscure *National Review,* that raise the question: what was wrong with the decisions of the 1920s, and do they not have something to teach us? Those decisions banned almost all immigration from Asia, and limited immigration from the eligible countries of the Eastern Hemisphere (almost all European) to 150,000 a year. Most of that was reserved for the British Isles and Germany: Southern and Eastern European countries—the source of most immigration at the time—were limited to tiny quotas. We see this act now as racist in its preference for whites and discriminatory in its preference for Protestant countries and its sharp restrictions on the countries from which Jewish immigrants then came. It was also considered anti-Catholic, although Catholics could come in under the ample quotas for Ireland and Germany.

But we can phrase the intentions of the 1924 act in quite another way: it said that what America was in 1920, in terms of ethnic and racial makeup, was in some way normative, and to be preferred to what it would become in the absence of immigration restriction; and it said that the United States was no longer to be a country of mass immigration. The 1924 law called for a remarkable scholarly exercise to determine the national origins of the white population: each country would have a share in the quota of 150,000 proportional to its contribution to the makeup of the white population. That this system prevailed, with modifications, for forty years suggests that the opposition to it, while impassioned, did not have much political power.

Despite the refugee crisis of the 1930s and the displaced

persons crisis of the post–World War II period, it survived: the McCarran-Walter Act of 1952 made little change in the overall pattern. The consensus of 1924 was finally swept away in 1965. The coalition that forced the abandonment of the arrangement of 1924 consisted of Jews, Catholics, and liberals, who had for years fought against the preferences for northwestern Europe and the restrictions on Asia. The new immigration act abandoned all efforts to make distinctions among nations on grounds of race, size, or historical connection. All would in principle be limited to a maximum of 20,000, under an overall cap of 290,000.

The dominating principles of the 1965 act were family connections and no discrimination on grounds of national origin. Italians, Poles, Greeks, or Jews would not be limited by highly restrictive quotas in their ability to enter the United States to join relatives; Asians would no longer be limited to minuscule quotas. But the government expected no great change in the volume or ethnic and racial character of immigration.

As it happens, there were not many Jews left in Europe who wanted to come or who could leave, even though Jewish organizations and members of Congress led the fight for a freer immigration policy. European prosperity soon reduced the number of Europeans who wanted to come; Communist rule restricted the number of Eastern Europeans who could come. Quite soon the composition of immigration changed from overwhelmingly European to overwhelmingly Asian, Latin American, and Caribbean. This was unintended and unexpected, but it was accepted. It played no role in the next great effort to fix immigration in the late 1970s. No one raised the question of why immigration to a country that had been settled by Europeans now included so few Europeans. The new immigration issue of the late 1970s was illegal immigration, primarily from Mexico.

A major immigration commission was set up in 1978. Its recommendations were incorporated into the Simpson-Mazzoli Immigration Reform Act of 1981, whose descendant finally became law as the Immigration Reform and Control Act of 1986. That act addressed the illegal immigration issue with a deal: those already here could apply, with restrictions, to legalize their status, but further numbers of illegal immigrants would be stanched by imposing penalties on employers who hired illegal immigrants.

In a few years further modifications were necessary. The new problem was that an immigration law oriented toward family preference meant preference for recent immigrants' relatives, those still linked by family connection to their emigrating relatives. This meant we would have few Europeans, who had immigrated a long time ago, and many Asians and Latin Americans. Congress tried to deal with this through lotteries. But the lotteries could not be for Europeans alone; they had to include a host of "underrepresented" nations.

Yet another issue that became evident under the settlement of 1965, and the changes of 1986, was that the numbers of immigrants who had family preference limited those who might enter with valuable skills in short supply in the United States, such as highly skilled machinists. And so the last major modification in the 1990 immigration law increased the number of those who could enter on the basis of needed skills. But it was not possible politically to reduce the number who came on the basis of family relationship, so the total number of allowable immigrants was raised. This is the kind of compromise that might surprise most Americans, if they knew about it. The total number of immigrants who can enter legally is now 700,000 (to which must be added 130,000 or so refugees, who came in under a separate allotment, and those seeking asylum).

So we move from crisis to crisis, or at least from problem to problem. The next crisis, already upon us, is the specific impact of large numbers of immigrants on the major cities that attract them: Los Angeles, New York, and Miami, preeminently. Here the issue is local costs, particularly for schools, hospitals, and welfare services—costs that are inevitable when population rises. New York City reports that it added 65,000 immigrant children to its schools in 1992–93, and 46,000 in 1991–92.

This issue of immigration's cost is rather complicated. The immigrant population, despite the popular image, is not one of greater needs and lesser capacities than the American population. Rather, the immigrants are divided between those who come in with educational and work qualifications higher than those of the average American (most of the Asians) and those who come in with educational and work qualifications lower than those of the average American (mostly Hispanics and people from Caribbean countries).

And even within these large categories there are great differences by national origin. Some groups show a higher proportion on welfare than the American average (though almost none shows as high a proportion as American blacks and Puerto Ricans), and some show a considerably lower proportion. Immigrants work and provide money to cities, states, and the federal government in taxes. Many work in hospitals as doctors and nurses and technicians, provide health services in underserved areas, do important research and teaching in universities and colleges. So how do we reckon up the balance? And is this the balance we should reckon?

In our efforts to determine just what kind of immigration policy we should have, we resort eagerly to the calculations of economists. But there is no clear guidance there. Julian Simon claims that people are always an economic asset: increasing the number of people increases the numbers of consumers and producers. Other economists are doubtful that labor with poor qualifications is much of a benefit. Some point out that low-wage industries (garment manufacturing, for example) would go overseas in even greater proportion without low-paid immigrant labor. Others argue it should: why is the most advanced economy in the world holding on to industries that have to compete with low-wage, developing countries? Some wonder who will provide service in restaurants and hotels, clean office buildings, take care of the children of high-paid professionals. Others point out that Japan manages to run hotels and restaurants with very few immigrants.

I have concluded that economics in general can give no large answer as to what the immigration policy of a nation should be. At the margin, one would think, where the good effects clearly are evident, economic considerations must prevail. But I recall an Australian economist confidently pronouncing the end of the Japanese miracle in a talk in Tokyo in 1962. Why? Because Japan could not or would not, for reasons of culture or xenophobia, import labor, as Europe was then doing, and labor shortages would call a halt to Japanese economic growth. Clearly, he had it wrong. The Japanese did not import labor, but did manage to maintain phenomenal economic growth.

But if not economics, then what? Politics? Culture? Here we move on to murky and dangerous ground. Thinking of the economist's comments on Japan in the 1960s, and contrasting suspicious and closed Japan with open Europe, then recruiting Yugoslavs and Turks, one wonders whether Europeans would now agree that their course was better. Immigration and the fates of the workers recruited from distant cultures and their children have become a permanent part of Europe's politics, spawning an ugly nativism there similar to that which closed America's borders in the 1920s.

This is no argument for the United States in its thinking about immigration, one might say. We are used to greater differences than the more homogeneous countries of Europe. We are a nation based not on a common ethnic stock linked by "mystic chords of memory," connection, kinship, but rather by common universal ideas. But I am not sure how deeply rooted this view is among Americans in general. We all know the power of the sense of kinship, real or mythical, in keeping people together—or in tearing them apart. (This possibility is exacerbated by our affirmative action policies, which, while designed to advance those American racial and ethnic groups that have suffered from and suffer still from discrimination, are not limited to citizens or legal residents.)

The present-day restrictionist movement deploys the economic arguments, but it is the others that really drive it. Much of its current modest strength comes from the heirs of the Zero Population Growth movement and from environmentalists who argue that there are already too many Americans. But an equally strong motivation of the movement comes from the sense that there was—is—an American culture that is threatened by too great a diversity. It is harder to make this argument publicly, for obvious reasons, since the question comes up: how do you define this American culture? Should it be or remain Christian or white or European?

The two kinds of argument are closely related. There are many Americans who regret the loss of a less crowded country and a more homogeneous culture. We are too prone to label them racists. There are indeed racists and bigots, and the restrictionist movement will undoubtedly attract them in number. Yet the motives I have pointed to among the current restrictionists, an attachment to a country more like what it once was, a preference for a less populated country, are not ignoble.

We go very far these days in testing motives for racism, if their effect is to bear differentially on ethnic and racial groups. It is true that a lower level of immigration, more preference for those with needed skills, a spin in favor of the "underrepresented," would all mean more Europeans, fewer Hispanics and Caribbeans and Asians. But the effects of such policies are not an index to the motives of those who advocate them. Nor would I call a motive that would prefer an immigrant stream closer in racial and ethnic character to the present composition of the American population necessarily racist. In British immigration law there is a category of "patrials"—persons born of British stock in other countries whose status is defined by ancestry, connection to Britain through parents or grandparents. In Germany, people of German origin, no matter how distant, have claims to immigration others do not. Israel has its "law of return"—which was the ground on which the country was labeled "racist." I would not describe any of these policies as racist: there is a difference between recognizing those who are in some sense one's own, with links to a people and a culture, and a policy based on dislike, hostility, or racial antagonism.

One other element should be mentioned as making up part of the immigration restriction movement. One finds in it children of immigrants, and immigrants themselves, who admire the ability of America to assimilate immigrants and their children, but who fear that the assimilatory powers of America have weakened because of the legal support to bilingualism in education and voting, because of the power of multicultural trends in education. It is easy to accuse such people of wanting to pull up the drawbridge after they have gained entry. They would answer that they fear the United States is no longer capable of assimilating those now coming as it assimilated them.

Is this a fair argument, or have the aging immigrants of the last great European wave and their children who may be found active in immigration restriction simply adopted the nativist prejudices of those who tried to bar them? But it *is* a different country: less self-confident, less willing to impose English and American customs and loyalty as simply the best in the world. We do not know whether this change in national mood and in educational philosophy and practice actually affects the rate at which immigrants assimilate, and which would depend on giving an answer as to what we mean by assimilation. Learning English? I do not think the new immigrants learn English at a slower rate than the older European immigrants. Taking up citizenship? This has always varied depending on the ethnic group. One sees the same variation among current immigrants, and if fewer become citizens one reason may be that there are now fewer advantages to citizenship as civil rights law spreads to protect aliens.

One even finds some anti-immigrant sentiment among the newest, post-1965 immigrants. This sentiment is directed primarily at illegal immigrants: it is exacerbated by the fact that there may be competition for jobs between older legal and newer illegal immigrants working at the same jobs. They may also share the same section of the city, and the older immigrants may see the new illegals contributing to neighborhood decline.

In time, American blacks may be numbered among the restrictionists. If there is indeed competition between immigrants, legal or illegal, and Americans, blacks are likely to be more affected than any other group. Up to now, the dream of the Rainbow Coalition has kept black members of Congress in the pro-immigration camp. I doubt that this reflects the dominant view among blacks.

My sense is that the state of American public opinion is now modestly restrictionist. The scale of immigration is larger than most people would choose, for a host of reasons: they don't think America should become a country of mass immigration again, and see no good reason, economic or other, for this. They ask why the stream of immigration should be so unrepresentative of the nation that already exists. They support the need to admit refugees. They are against illegal immigration, even though they may benefit from the services of such immigrants. They think immigration policies should reflect our compassion (refugees), our respect for human rights (asylum seekers), the desire of immigrant neighbors to bring in parents, children, and spouses, perhaps some brothers and sisters. They believe immigration policies should reflect our desire to improve the country—more of the kind of immigrants who become high school class valedictorians and win science prizes.

That is about where I come out, too. There is no blueprint here, only a list of preferences that are not disreputable and should be respected. Whatever our policies are, however, I think our biggest problem will be to carry them out in a world in which so many see entry into the United States as a way of improving themselves.

How different would that be from what we have? When one considers present immigration policies, it seems we have insensibly reverted to mass immigration, without ever having made a decision to do so. Few Americans believe our population is too low, our land too lightly settled, our resources unexploited, our industries and commerce short of labor. But our politics, the result of various pressures operating within a framework of decent and generous ideals, end up looking as if we believe all this is true. The pressures consist of recent immigrants who want to bring in family members (no small group—there were eight million immigrants in the 1980s), agricultural interests that want cheap labor, a Hispanic caucus that believes any immigration restriction demeans Hispanics, foreign policy interests that require us to take a substantial number of refugees, and civil rights groups that expand the rights of illegal immigrants, refugees, and asylum seekers.

These interests are not necessarily distinguishable from ideals of generosity toward those in desperate need, compassion for those who simply seek a country with more opportunity, and respect for a tradition, rather recently reminted, that asserts we are a nation of immigrants, should remain so, and should be proud of it.

The fulfillment of these ideals does not, however, suggest that there are any moral and ethical imperatives that dictate we have no right to make the decision that the United States, as it stands, with all its faults, is what we prefer to the alternative that would be created by mass immigration. The United States can survive without large numbers of low-skilled workers, and would probably survive, if it was so inclined, without highly trained foreign engineers, doctors, and scientists. At the level of the highest skills and talents we will undoubtedly always be happy to welcome immigrants—we did even in the restrictive 1930s and 1940s. In a world in which masses of people can move, or be moved, too easily beyond their native borders, we will always need policies to set limits as to what the responsibilities of this country are.

There is one kind of immigration restriction on which all (in theory) agree, and that is control of illegal immigration. Much would be required to stem it, and the 1986 act did not. We would need identity documents more resistant to forgery, more Border Patrol officers, better qualified investigators of claims to asylum, and much more. The effort to control illegal immigration will be expensive if it is to be effective. We may be able to learn from the European countries now trying to stem illegal immigration. A stronger effort to reduce illegal immigration may serve as a prelude to a more effective immigration regime generally, and that will be task enough for the next few years. Or we may discover in the effort that such control requires measures that we simply don't want to live with. It will be valuable to learn that, too.

Immigration Dilemmas
Richard Rothstein

Richard Rothstein is a research associate at the Economic Policy Institute in Washington, D.C. He writes a bimonthly column for the *L.A. Weekly* and *La Opinion*. "Immigration Dilemmas" first appeared in *Dissent,* Fall 1993.

DURING THE PRESIDENTIAL campaign, Bill Clinton delivered a foreign policy speech in Los Angeles; the first question from the audience was a predictable, "Who are your foreign policy advisers going to be?" Clinton demurred, calling such considerations premature. Next, a questioner asked the candidate what he proposed to do about illegal immigration. Clinton said he didn't know what to do, since immigration is the most complex issue facing the nation. "If you have an answer," Clinton told the questioner, "*you* can be my foreign policy adviser!" It may have been the first time the "policy-wonk" candidate couldn't come up with a ready solution.

The impossibility of border control is the most obvious difficulty. The Coast Guard can't effectively police every mile of our coastline; the occasional interception of a Chinese human cargo ship is only token. We now have over three thousand federal agents patrolling two thousand miles of the U.S.-Mexican land border, also with little success. Last year, the Border Patrol intercepted 1.2 million would-be immigrants from Mexico, but since there is no point to incarcerating them (or jail space to do so), nearly all are sent back to try again; 100,000 to 600,000 a year evade capture. So if the intercepted ones keep trying, the odds are increasingly in their favor.

Giving up on border control is no solution either. Open contempt for any important law engenders disrespect for the law itself, so we owe it to our national integrity to make serious attempts at enforcement. Also, setting aside for the moment the complicated question of whether newcomers compete with native workers for jobs, it is indisputable that undocumented immigrants who take jobs in labor-short occupations deny places to would-be lawful immigrants who live in nations from which illegal entry is less practical. It is to these equally desperate and ambitious migrants that our ineffective border control is most unfair.

When we attempted to rescue respect for law by abandoning our fifty-five-miles-per-hour speed limit in rural areas because most people flouted it, we established a new limit of sixty-five mph, a level we thought drivers would respect. But for illegal immigration, there is no analogous solution, because the most sophisticated analysts can't make a reasonable guess at the level of immigration that must be allowed before control is practical. Even today's educated guess could change tomorrow, based on political developments abroad (like the Tiananmen massacre or the overthrow of Aristide) or changes in economic growth rates and job creation in places like Mexico and the Dominican Republic. The reality would also change with job opportunities here. Fewer immigrants would come if they knew there was no work awaiting them; even in poor countries, people rarely want to leave their families and communities. It's not that the pressure for illegal immigration is so great that if we relaxed our barriers, we'd be inundated with hordes of immigrants. Though nobody knows how many Mexicans would actually immigrate if they could do so unimpeded, the number is smaller than most Americans think. Early in this century, when Mexicans were even poorer relative to Americans than they are today, American railroads and farmers had to send recruiters to Mexico to beg laborers to come.

In Europe, experts feared there would be massive migration of poor Italians to high-wage countries like France and Germany when the European Community (EC) was established, so Italian emigration was restricted. When restrictions were finally abandoned in 1968, however, few Italians left home. The wage differential between Germany and Italy was still four to one, but for most Italians, the income difference wasn't great enough to make the upheaval worthwhile. Today, despite continuing income differences between countries like Ireland, Spain, Greece, and Italy, on the one hand, and France and Germany on the other, only 1.5 percent of the EC's population was born in a different EC country from the one in which they now reside. The EC has lots of immigrants—but most come from poorer countries in Africa, Eastern Europe, and the Middle East.

Americans who are frustrated with our country's inability to regulate immigration might reflect on the experience of other industrial nations, even those with less inclusive traditions. Japan, for example, with its aging workforce and declining fertility rate, also has a need for low-wage immigrants, even now in a stagnant economy. Since 1989 Japan has crafted a temporary, and racist, solution by recruiting some 200,000 (according to official government figures) South American workers who have partial Japanese ancestry. But professional smuggling rings are already at work importing South Americans with documents faking Japanese bloodlines. As immigration expert Wayne Cornelius points out, of the 30,000 Peruvians now in Japan, half may be illegal. In addition to those counted in official data, there may be as many as 250,000 Brazilians who came to Japan as "tourists" and then stayed on to work. Japan also has illegal immigrants from Malaysia, Thailand, Iran, Bangladesh, and Pakistan who overstayed tourist visas. And there are 700,000 Koreans living in Japan, many descended from laborers imported by force during Japan's prewar occupation of Korea, others who immigrated illegally in recent years. The sociologist Nathan Glazer has remarked that one does not note in Japan, a country with very few immigrants, unmade hotel beds, unwashed dishes in restaurants, unmanned filling stations. "It seems there is a way of managing even without immigrants." Glazer should look again. In 1992 alone, 280,000 foreigners came to Japan on short-term visas and then disappeared into the country.

And then there is France, whose new conservative government proclaims a goal of "zero immigration." It's a fantasy. There are already one million undocumented immigrants living in France, with another 4.5 million immigrants there illegally—mostly Algerians, Moroccans, and Tunisians. All told, immigrants make up over 10 percent of France's population, and many have relatives and friends who are ready to join them, legally or illegally.

Last year, one thousand would-be immigrants drowned while trying to swim to Spain. Uncounted others made it, ferried to a point two hundred yards from shore by Moroccan smugglers. In return for a promise of $2 billion in aid from the EC, Morocco has now agreed to station 3,500 troops on its beaches to try to deter human smuggling, yet the illegal immigration continues. In Germany there are nearly two million Turkish immigrants, brought into the country over a thirty-year period as "guest workers," who never went home. All told, there are probably five million undocumented immigrants in Western Europe, 1.5 percent of the population. In the United States, there are perhaps three and a half million undocumenteds, a slightly smaller share of our population, though we have another three million formerly undocumented persons who were "legalized" after the 1986 amnesty. Our self-image of America as a nation uniquely open to immigration is historically accurate but less true today. Although our immigration restrictionists are now more civilized than those in Germany, the 8.5 percent of our population that is foreign-born is not much greater than the 8.2 percent of German residents who came from elsewhere. In 1920, however, over 13 percent of Americans were foreign-born. *Then* we were unique, but not now, when throughout the world one hundred million people are immigrants in one country or another.

Push and Pull

All industrialized nations have an "immigration problem" for similar reasons. When labor markets are tight or we want agricultural or service work performed cheaply, we welcome immigrants, sometimes without restriction, sometimes through official "guest worker" programs. But bringing guest workers into a country is easier than sending them home. Once they arrive, it is virtually impossible to prevent them from leaving the jobs for which they were recruited and finding other work.

It used to be easier to send immigrants back when their work was done, because their wives were content to wait for them at home. But many Mexican women, for example, are no longer willing to stay home while their husbands travel back and forth to earn money in the United States. Now, women want to come north to work as well, either with their husbands or independently. Since 1987 alone, the number of Mexican women attempting to cross the border illegally has doubled, while the number of men has not changed. A consequence is declining return migration for men.

Once an immigration group establishes a presence, networks linking immigrants with their home country become difficult to break. In the United States, we give priority for legal immigration to "family reunification," meaning that immigrants can bring their relatives here at the head of the line. For example, workers amnestied under the 1986 law will soon be eligible to bring in family members—several million additional legal residents.

Few immigrants leave home without some idea of how to

find work in America. Once an immigrant community is established here, this becomes a lot easier. Immigrants recruit friends and relatives from back home when their employers need additional help. In the garment districts of Los Angeles, New York, or Miami, entire plants are staffed by immigrants from the same small village in Mexico, El Salvador, or China. Once such powerful networks are established, policy is impotent to break them.

When George Bush and Carlos Salinas first began promoting the North American Free Trade Agreement (NAFTA), one of their claims was that providing more jobs in Mexico would reduce the Mexicans' desire to emigrate. The claim is heard less frequently now because it has become clear that the relationship is more complex. Emigration is expensive (the illegal kind often requires hiring a guide and buying false documents for as much as $2,000), and the poorest Mexicans can't afford it. If Mexico becomes more prosperous, more people will have money to pay for emigration.

Traditional societies send few emigrants, but the disruption of traditional ways spurs emigration. As countries industrialize, formerly rural workers, now more rootless, begin to think of the next step—emigration. Industrial workers aspire to better jobs, and when they reach the limit of their upward mobility at home, think of the next step— emigration. Undocumented Mexican immigrants are almost never those without jobs at home; they have above-average education and aspirations whetted by urban industrial employment. In the 1970s, South Korea's economy was the fastest growing in the world, and its emigration rate to the United States was also the fastest growing.

Today, the ratio of U.S. to Mexican wages is about seven to one, and the ratio of living standards (measured purchasing power) is about three to one. As this gap narrows, economic growth and development in Mexico will initially stimulate *increased* migration to the United States. At some point in the future, most experts believe, the gap will become small enough that emigration will slow. But nobody can hazard a guess about when that point might come—one U.S. government commission recently concluded it could take "several generations." Something short of full equality with U.S. incomes is necessary. Few Americans, after all, move from city to city in search of relatively small wage increases, so long as they have a job at home. Mexicans are even less likely to abandon their culture and homeland for small income differences. As noted earlier, a four-to-one ratio wasn't enough to spur Italian moves to Germany.

Immigration flows are even more immune to policy influences because the relationship between economic status at home and the propensity to migrate varies from society to society and from time to time. By 1980, one-third of working-age persons born in Puerto Rico had migrated to the mainland. The migrants were Puerto Ricans with below-average education levels, and they were more likely to be unemployed before leaving the island—just the opposite of today's Mexican immigrants. Why? According to economists Alida Castillo-Freeman and Richard Freeman, it is because Congress raised Puerto Rico's minimum wage so high that island unemployment increased; for the remaining jobs, employers were able to select only the most qualified workers, who then chose not to migrate and accepted relatively good pay at home. Those left on the streets migrated. By establishing a high minimum wage for Puerto Rico, Congress in effect determined that it was better to bring unskilled Puerto Rican migrants to New York than to send New York jobs to Puerto Rico. Had the Puerto Rican minimum wage been lower, fewer islanders would have migrated, but more factories would have left the mainland for the island's low-wage haven. Can we conclude from the Puerto Rican experience that Mexican migration will slow if Mexican wages are kept low? No: too many other factors will intervene.

In reality, NAFTA and trade policy could become irrelevant to the volume of future immigration flows from Mexico, since, as Wayne Cornelius suggests, these factors are likely to be swamped by Mexico's domestic agriculture policy. Before President Salinas's policies of economic liberalization, Mexico subsidized peasants to remain in rural areas; the government, for example, bought corn from peasants at twice the world price and prohibited the sale of communal farmlands to private investors. But last year the Mexican constitution was amended to permit these lands to be sold, and it is widely expected that corn and bean subsidies will decline. The purpose of these policies is to encourage investment in efficient cash crops for export, but if successful, they will result in many fewer peasants working the land: approximately one million peasants are expected to leave farming annually during the next ten to twenty years. The Mexican labor force is already growing at the rate of one million job seekers per year, from three hundred thousand to half a million more than current economic growth can absorb. Emigration pressures will be irresistible, regardless of NAFTA or U.S. border policies.

Paying for Our Pensions

Two claims fuel much of the recent debate about immigration. One is that immigrants draw more on public services (like welfare and public health) than they contribute in taxes. The second is that immigrants take jobs from the rest of us.

It is true that local government is burdened by immigrant services. Over 10 percent of California's immigrants are on welfare, and over 25 percent of southern California's jail population are immigrants. But at the same time, our national budget is becoming more dependent on immigrant taxes. Fewer Americans will be working when the baby-boom generation (born between 1946 and 1964) begins to reach retirement age in 2010. By that time, we will have spent the boomers' Social Security contributions to offset the federal budget deficit. So we'll need the taxes of younger working immigrants to pay Medicare and Social Security for the older generation. The services-taxes balance of which we now complain will become a national, not a local issue. And immigrants will become part of the solution, not the problem.

Today, 12 percent of Americans are over sixty-five years old, and their health and retirement benefits consume about one-third of all federal spending. When the baby-boom generation retires, 20 percent will be over sixty-five. No longer paying income or Social Security taxes, they will instead consume Social Security and Medicare. These benefits can be paid for only by large tax increases on those still working, by big jumps in productivity, or by changes in the ratio of working to retired Americans.

We can improve the ratio if we make people work longer and raise their retirement age. Minor steps have already been taken: the normal retirement age for Social Security will be raised to sixty-seven in 2027, and further increases are inevitable. We can also improve the ratio with an increase in birth rates, so that more young workers are available to replace those who retire. This is also happening: the fertility rate (children borne by the average woman) has jumped from 1.87 to 2.05 in the last five years. But this is not something we necessarily want to encourage; it contradicts, for example, our desire to reduce teen pregnancies.

Ultimately, we can't increase the working-to-retired ratio enough without a lot more immigration. While only 26 percent of the U.S. population is now in the prime working age of twenty to thirty-nine, 46 percent of immigrants are in that age group. Retiring baby boomers need people who contribute more in taxes than they consume in services. Immigration will have to be an increasing part of the solution, not only in the United States, but throughout the industrial world. Germans now retire at age sixty, but the sixty-and-over set, now 21 percent of Germany's population, will make up 30 percent by the year 2020. With fewer workers to pay that many pensions, Germany has increased its retirement age to sixty-five, effective in 2012. Germany needs more young Turks, not fewer. Japan's fertility rate is only 1.53 and, in thirteen years, Japan is expected to become the first country in the world where over 20 percent of the population is older than sixty-five, a point the United States can expect to reach by 2025, unless there is a lot more immigration.

Competition for Jobs

Do immigrants take jobs from residents? In some cases they do and in others they provide labor no native group is willing to supply. It is impossible to design an immigration policy that bars the "takers" and welcomes the "providers."

Important industries (garment manufacturing, for example) could not exist without an immigrant labor supply; no native workers are available or willing to work in these industries even in periods of high unemployment. If natives were willing to work, they would demand wage-and-benefit packages that would certainly make the industries uncompetitive with companies based abroad. Our minimum wage is now so low, however, that lawful employers can survive by paying the minimum to immigrant workers, while sweatshop operators exploit immigrants' vulnerability and collect an additional premium. Because of immigrant seamstresses, an industry exists that supports not only its professional and managerial employees but a variety of upstream workers in computer software, machine tools, textiles, and petrochemicals. In Los Angeles, with mostly undocumented immigrant workers, the garment industry has grown in the last decade, while manufacturing as a whole, and especially garment manufacturing, has declined nationwide.

There is also no displacement of native workers in low-wage service jobs, in restaurant kitchens, say, or hotels. It is, of course, theoretically possible that restaurants and hotels could be forced to pay wages high enough to attract American high school graduates, but if they did so, we'd have many fewer (because much more expensive) vacations and conventions, not to mention meals away from home.

American upper-middle-class life is dependent on immigrant workers performing tasks at wages no established resident would consider. Zoë Baird didn't need to hire an illegal immigrant to care for her child; she could have afforded to pay good wages. But most two-job families or single parents are not in Baird's income class. Immigrant wages for housecleaning, lawn mowing, child care, and even car washing make work outside the home feasible for people who could otherwise not afford it. Those who dream of cities without poorly educated, low-wage immigrants should be required to describe what middle-class and even lower-middle-class life would be like without them. It can't be done, but the fantasy persists that a policy could be devised that welcomes the restaurant, hotel, and personal service workers on whom we obviously depend, but bans all others.

Another important industry that could not exist but for immigrants is horticulture. In a way, George Bush's inability to banish broccoli from health-conscious American diets is one cause of undocumented immigration. Harvest of corn, wheat, and other grains is mechanized, but fruit, vegetable, and nut horticulture, occupying only 1 percent of U.S. farmland, is labor-intensive and consumes 40 percent of total farm wages. A broccoli crop, for example, requires fifty-two labor-hours per acre. According to agricultural economists Phil Martin and Edward Taylor, U.S. acreage devoted to broccoli increased by 50 percent in the 1980s as Americans' annual fresh broccoli consumption almost tripled to 4.5 pounds per person. Broccoli alone brought two thousand migrant farmworkers from rural Mexico to the United States. Other healthy fruits and vegetables had a similar impact; fresh tomato consumption jumped from thirteen to eighteen pounds per person, and U.S. production grew by 38 percent. Production of all vegetables combined rose by

33 percent, because even imports from countries like Mexico and Chile couldn't satiate Americans' hunger for more vitamins and roughage. Besides, Latin Americans also want to stay healthy. Carlos Salinas's goal of "exporting tomatoes, not tomato pickers" is frustrated by Mexicans' consumption of tomatoes at twice the per-capita rate of Americans. Even rapid expansion of Mexican tomato acreage won't replace U.S. growers' demands for immigrant labor.

Bush did make something of a contribution to solving the problem. Since fresh-vegetable consumption rises with upscale lifestyles, holding down personal income growth kept vegetable acreage from increasing even more than it did. Martin and Taylor report that fresh vegetables have high "elasticities"; in other words, a 1 percent increase in family income is associated with a 1 percent increase in broccoli and lettuce consumption and a 2.4 percent increase for cauliflower. So if the Clinton administration succeeds in reversing the trend of declining family income, Americans will eat even more veggies, requiring more rural immigrants, legal or not.

Factoring these kinds of variables into rational immigration rules is beyond the ability of any policymaker. We can let migrant workers in as the demand for vegetables expands, but how do we reduce the number of "guests" when demand contracts, and how can we require them to avoid enticing their brothers and cousins to join them? Communist governments were mostly successful at preventing workers from being employed without authorization but no other governments have been able to do so.

There are also industries where immigrants do compete with natives, and this competition not only creates native unemployment but reduces wages for those who remain at work as well. Here's one example: fifteen years ago, residential drywallers—the people who erect plasterboard for interior home walls—were represented by the carpenters' union in southern California. They averaged about $1,100 in weekly earnings, in today's dollars. Union drywall agreements required homebuilders to pay for full family health insurance. Each employer contributed to a vacation and pension fund for each hour worked. But in the late 1970s, contractors began to hire Mexican immigrants to work without union contract protection. Immigrant workers in turn recruited their friends and relatives, and by 1982 enough nonunion drywallers (many from just one town in rural Mexico) were available, and the contractors stopped hiring union labor altogether. With the carpenters' union out of the picture, contractors also dropped their health insurance plans, stopped paying into vacation and pension funds, and cut wages. Contractors now dealt only with labor brokers who paid workers in cash and ignored income-tax withholding, Social Security, unemployment insurance, and minimum-wage laws. By 1992, drywallers worked nearly sixty hours a week to take home $300 in cash, with no benefits. In an atypical action, these undocumented immigrant construction workers went on strike to bring back the carpenters' union. A clever union lawyer went after the contractors for minimum-wage violations and used the potential back-pay liability to leverage a strike settlement that included reinstatement of health insurance and a wage increase. Drywallers now earn about double what they got before the strike, and about half what nonimmigrant workers earned a decade earlier.

The construction industry where immigrants displaced native workers and the vegetable industry where no natives choose to work are extreme ends on a scale of displacement. Advocates of loosening border controls cite the former; advocates of tightening cite the latter. Some industries, like garment, can be cited by each. Fifteen years ago, undocumented immigrants fully displaced African-American garment workers in many cities, because the immigrants were willing to tolerate wages and conditions far below what legal workers were used to. In Los Angeles, for example, fifty-five thousand native garment workers were displaced by immigrants in the 1970s. But today, international competition in garment assembly has become so fierce that a domestic industry probably could not survive if it paid the wages of fifteen years ago. Can immigrants, therefore, be said to have displaced African-American workers in the garment industry? Yes and no.

Today it's probably the case that more immigrants are working in jobs natives don't want than in competitive occupations. But even though laid-off aerospace engineers don't normally seek work as gardeners or car washers, this is a hard argument to make when unemployment is high and wages are declining. And the argument will become even harder if the proposals of some reformers—to increase the immigration of skilled workers—become law. Expanding legal immigration quotas for professional and technical workers will certainly increase competition for scarce jobs.

Solutions

Total border control is an unrealizable dream; it is impossible to calculate immigration flows to match domestic employment needs; and a variety of uncontrollable and unpredictable economic, political, and social developments in sending countries will, in any event, have a lot to do with the actual level of immigration. As candidate Clinton realized, we can't hope to design a coherent immigration policy. But there are piecemeal policies we can implement that address some of the problems, at least around the edges.

These reforms might, if we are lucky, combine with other political and economic developments to slow the "push" of immigrants from sending countries, provide some additional protection for native workers in those few industries where competition with immigrants is a reality, and encourage more honorable and responsible treatment of immigrants, who, in any event, will continue to arrive. It's not that stepped-up border patrols are entirely useless; it's just that we shouldn't delude ourselves into believing that massive national and international political and economic forces can be reversed by more vigilant policing.

One important reform would be a Mexican development program that goes beyond free trade. If we truly want less Mexican immigration, persuading the Mexican government to slow its agricultural liberalization would be one approach. Failing that, we could underwrite targeted industrial policy in Mexico, which, in violation of free trade rules, would subsidize the development of small industries in rural areas where peasants are being displaced. Funds spent in this way might be more effective than hiring more Border Patrol agents.

Similarly, a more aggressive and earlier defense of Haiti's democratic government was, in retrospect, the only sensible (and morally decent) immigration policy we could have adopted with regard to that country's boat people. The civil wars in Central America and Indochina, whatever else they might have been, will ultimately have affected America most by raising immigration flows—as any tour through Salvadoran, Vietnamese, and Cambodian communities in California will attest. But these likely results are rarely considered when foreign policy is fashioned.

Better labor standards enforced in this country would also address parts of the problem. If labor law had been reformed so it wasn't so easy for construction contractors to abandon their contractual relationships with trade unions, it might have been more difficult for immigrants to displace union members in California's homebuilding industry. Enforcement of minimum-wage, health and safety, and other workplace rules could reduce, albeit only marginally, incentives for employers to substitute immigrants for natives in other industries where real competition takes place.

Higher labor standards in immigrant industries where native workers don't choose to work would also ameliorate political conflict over the unavoidable presence of undocumented workers. A national health insurance plan, for example, that covered all workers whether here legally or not would relieve the burden of taxpayers to provide for immigrant health in public emergency rooms and hospitals. Minimum-wage enforcement in immigrant industries, along with a more hospitable climate for union organizing, would put more money into immigrant neighborhoods and increase their tax contributions to the broader community, while reducing immigrant use of welfare, food stamp, and similar benefits.

And also, of course, we could stop eating broccoli.

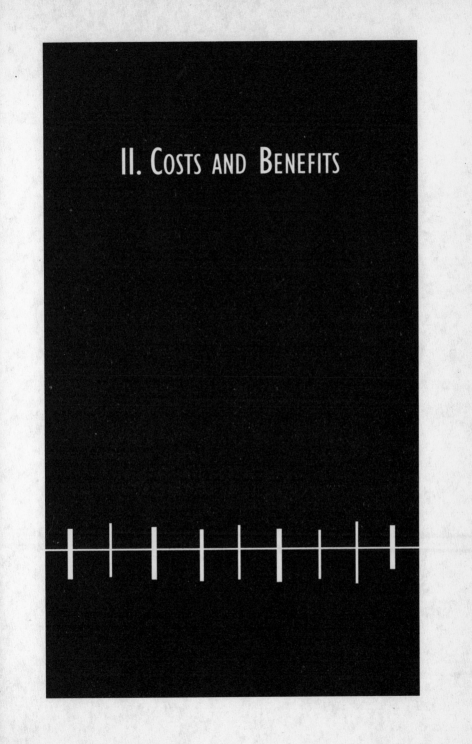

II. Costs and Benefits

Is Immigration Hurting the U.S.?
Jaclyn Fierman

Jaclyn Fierman is an associate editor of *Fortune*. She was previously associate editor for *World Business Weekly* and a reporter for the Commodity News Service. "Is Immigration Hurting the U.S.?" first appeared in *Fortune*, August 9, 1993.

A RECORD NINE million people immigrated to the United States in the 1980s, roughly equal to the number of tempest-tossed citizens now out of work and yearning to rejoin the labor market. This coincidence has not been lost on low-skilled Americans, who are competing for fewer jobs·at lower wages. But even many among the well-educated and highly paid have begun to wonder whether Lady Liberty should dim her beacon. As Cornell University labor economist Vernon Briggs puts it, "Why allow even one unskilled worker into this country when we have so many of our own?"

Fully 61 percent of respondents polled in June by the *New York Times* and CBS News said the nation's open-armed immigration policy should be curtailed. Congress is now considering several bills to stem a separate tide—the growing number of people seeking political asylum. Last year over 100,000 of these poured in; many disappeared permanently into the crowd after receiving temporary working papers and a date for a formal hearing. Immigration has also captured the attention of President Clinton, who says he plans to make the issue "a priority."

Such concern is global. In Europe, rising immigration at a time of record unemployment is expanding the ranks of right-wing parties and sparking ugly urban riots. Germany, which long boasted the Old World's most open borders, stopped hearing most new pleas for political asylum as of July 1.

While things aren't nearly so bad in the United States, recent events are fanning public anxiety. Islamic fundamentalists, some residing in the United States illegally, were among the suspects arrested in connection with the World Trade Center bombing and a later plot to blow up New York tunnels and buildings.* The wreck along New York City's coastline of a boat loaded with nearly three hundred illegal Chinese immigrants turned a spotlight on the booming Asian black market that smuggles foreigners (for hefty fees) into the United States.

What should be done? Obviously Washington can and must improve its efforts to keep out the truly dangerous. And while it's impossible to eliminate illegal immigration, the government also ought to ensure that the number of incoming illegals—perhaps as many as 300,000 annually in recent years—at least doesn't move higher and even begins to abate. Beyond that, however, U.S. immigration policy is basically sound and humane. There's no economic case for trimming back the current target of roughly 700,000 authorized immigrants a year, some 500,000 of whom are members of families being reunited. If anything, the United States should welcome *more* newcomers from especially desirable groups—namely, the gifted, the ambitious, and the rich.

How many more? In 1935 economist Bernhard Ostrolenk, a Polish immigrant, rejected the idea that new arrivals competed with Americans for a finite number of jobs: "The number is not fixed by some occult power, but increases with industrial activity."

---

*Since this article was written, a jury has convicted the men charged with bombing the World Trade Center.

Prescribing slightly higher legal immigration will inflame hotheads convinced that such a policy would damage the U.S. economy. But it's based on cold facts. The Urban Institute estimates that about 74 percent of adult male immigrants hold jobs, versus 72 percent of the general male population. Even illegals with limited education have acquitted themselves well. In 1986 the United States granted amnesty to three million illegal aliens, about two-thirds of whom were Mexican. Today, says economist Demetrios Papademetriou, chief immigration expert in the Bush administration, virtually all the adults are earning more than the minimum wage.

This relative paucity of freeloaders and deadbeats means that rookie Americans, as a group, more than pay their way. George Borjas, an economics professor at the University of California at San Diego, calculates that the nation's twenty million immigrants currently receive about $1.1 billion more in cash welfare payments each year than they pay into the welfare system through taxes. But by working and spending on things like food, rent, and clothing, they also contribute $5 billion annually to the economy. Net gain for the United States: almost $4 billion a year.

What about high unemployment among America's troubled urban underclass? Can't much of that be pinned on record levels of immigration? No, says Wade Henderson, director of the Washington, D.C., office of the National Association for the Advancement of Colored People: "You can't blame immigrants for the problems of the black poor." Their plight, he says, mainly arises from failures in domestic social policy rather than from immigration policy.

That's not to say that wrenching displacement never occurs. Janitors in Los Angeles and hotel workers in Washington, D.C., to select two instances, were once predominantly black Americans and are now mainly immigrants. But experts agree that in most cases new arrivals replace and compete for low-skilled jobs with other immigrants, not with Americans. The garment industry is a prime example: men and women from Latin America, the Caribbean, and the Far East sit at machines once operated by Italians and Jews. "The garment district has always been a stepping-stone for immigrants, especially those who speak no English," says Thomas Glubiak of New York State's Department of Labor.

Compelling evidence even shows that immigrants boost overall employment on balance. In a study of the four hundred largest U.S. counties, Maria Enchautegui, an economist at the Urban Institute, found that for every one-hundred-person increase in the population of adult immigrants, the number of new jobs rose by forty-six. By contrast, for every one hundred new native-born Americans, the number of jobs rose by just twenty-five.

Toy Town in Los Angeles demonstrates how immigrants can raise employment, revitalize neighborhoods, even expand global trade. Smack in the middle of L.A.'s version of the Bowery, some three hundred wholesalers sell over $1 billion a year in low-tech toys made in the Far East—blocks, guns, jump ropes, soldiers, dolls. The merchants were largely born in Taiwan, Hong Kong, and Vietnam, and arrived in the United States almost penniless. But the business required little English, and warehouse space in the area was cheap. Today Toy Town employs 2,000 people. Its entrepreneurs sell not only to toy outlets in the United States, but also to those in Mexico, Canada, and Eastern Europe.

Among the most successful is Charles Woo, forty-one, born in Hong Kong and partially paralyzed by a childhood bout with polio. In 1969 he came to the United States to study physics at U.C.L.A. Ten years later, on the verge of receiving his doctorate, he quit school to start ABC Toys with his brother, Shu. "We know what American kids want," he says. Five years ago he started a second wholesale company, Mega Toys, whose fifteen employees sell $15 million in goods a year.

Though immigration's long-term benefits are compelling, the short-term adjustment costs can be high, particularly since the task of absorbing one million people a year is not evenly distributed across the country. It falls hardest on six cities: Los Angeles, New York, Chicago, Houston, Washington, and Miami. While illegals don't qualify for, say, food stamps or welfare payments, every youngster living in the United States is entitled by law to an education, regardless of the family's immigration status. Likewise, public hospitals, despite acute overcrowding and underfunding, must be blind when responding to medical emergencies.

Record inflows of refugees, immigrants, and illegals have forced the overburdened to go begging. California governor Pete Wilson has asked Washington for $1.45 billion to cover immigrant expenses. New York has asked the federal government to take custody of the three thousand illegal aliens crowding state jails at a cost of $65 million a year.

Others who have a right to feel shortchanged are the country's unskilled laborers. During the 1980s the gap between what they pocketed, on average, and what college graduates earned grew from 26 percent to 55 percent. This widening wage differential is mainly caused by rising competition from low-paid foreign workers who stay *at home*—and who are taking away market share in industries the United States once dominated. Still, Harvard economist Richard Freeman attributes about one-third of the gap to the fact that the ranks of willing but poorly educated workers were swelled by immigrants. However, the only sure-fire way to help displaced blue-collar Americans, he says, is through better education and training, not through immigration policy.

Even so, don't make the mistake of assuming that every last newcomer entering the country is short on book learning. Fully 25 percent of the arrivals in the 1980s had college degrees, according to the Urban Institute. The new American is someone around twenty-six years old, as likely to be male as female. He or she is an urban creature, apt to settle in an ethnic enclave along a public transportation line, and similar to the people *Harper's* magazine described in 1914: "America's attraction is not to the good or the bad, to the saint or to the sinner, but to the young, the aggressive, the restless, the ambitious."

What has changed is the skin color, culture, and language of immigrants. In the 1950s 53 percent of them came from Europe and just 6 percent from Asia. During the 1980s only 11 percent were European; most of the rest were evenly split between Asians and Latinos. Asians settled mainly in California; Latinos spread out.

Behind the geographic flip-flop was a sweeping immigration reform in the mid-1960s that redressed a long history of racist policy. Despite a sterling record—the United States currently admits more legal immigrants than all other potential host nations combined—the country has always been of two minds about coping with hordes of newcomers. Almost every poll ever published on the subject, and there have been dozens since the 1930s, shows that a majority of Americans—predominantly descendants of immigrants—favor further limits on immigration. Says Rita Simon, author of *The Ambivalent Welcome,* a new book on the subject: "It is something of a miracle that over fifty million immigrants gained entry to the U.S. between 1880 and 1990."

Swept up in the spirit of the civil rights movement, however, the United States in 1965 started to do away with quotas that favored white Europeans and made family reunification the pillar of its new policy. (Before, family ties carried less weight in decisions to grant entry.) In poured children, parents, spouses, and siblings from all parts of the world.

In 1990 Congress took another stab at immigration reform, this time with a more focused economic eye. The government nearly tripled to 140,000 the number of visas distributed on the basis of skills. Here's the breakdown: Skilled workers and their families get roughly 120,000 visas; the unskilled, 10,000. Another 10,000 visas are reserved for people willing to invest $1 million in the United States. Even among the half million visas handed out to unite families, don't assume the bulk go to unskilled workers. Most families are a mix. Tagging along behind Papa, who has a sixth-grade education, might be his son the rocket scientist.

When Washington revisits immigration policy, what talents should it favor? One of the most urgently needed might not strike some as a "skill." In the alphabet soup of categories, unskilled visas—classified EW, jokingly referred to as the Eternally Waiting group—include those for child care workers and home health aides. "The wait is sixteen years, time enough for that person to care for the next generation," says Theodore Ruthizer, a New York immigrant attorney. Ruthizer argues compellingly that foreign-born nannies and other caretakers ought to be able to work lawfully while they wait for their papers—a limbo that should be limited to three years. Washington might consider classifying these much-in-demand people as skilled workers. Any conscientious parent would agree with that designation.

The road for artists who uplift our spirits can be as tortuous as the one the unskilled must travel. German cinematographer Michael Ballhaus, fifty-seven, is valued in Hollywood for his ability to "shoot a $10 million movie on a $5 million budget," as he puts it. His credits include hits like Martin Scorsese's *Goodfellas* and Mike Nichols's *Working Girl*. But despite investing three years and $20,000 for immigration lawyers, Ballhaus was repeatedly denied a green card in the category reserved for gifted artists on grounds that his talents were technical, not artistic. In 1987 he—and 1.4 million others—entered the immigration sweepstakes, a quirky component of U.S. immigration law that now selects 40,000 winners a year. Ballhaus won his green card; Hollywood won, too.

America's ambivalence about welcoming the talented, the tired, and the poor even extends to the rich. The 1990 reform made a modest effort to change that, allocating 10,000 visas a year to foreigners willing to make at least a one-million-dollar investment (or $500,000 in depressed areas) and to hire ten Americans to work at the business. So far only 725 people have sought permanent residence by

this route. In 1993 the Immigration and Naturalization Service had approved 296 applications and rejected 140 by the
end of May, and was still weighing the rest.

One who knocked on this door is Taiwan's Tomi Huang,
forty-six. Huang started a tour bus company in California in
1991. She bought four buses for $300,000 each and employs
the requisite ten people, plus one. She rents out the buses—
complete with drivers who speak Spanish, English, or Chinese—to travel agents who in turn book foreign clients to
Disneyland, Las Vegas, and other West Coast attractions.
Huang, whose family owns a taxi company in Taiwan and
"half a mountainside" with fruit trees, says she started the
business after taking a bus tour herself. "It looked like fun,
and I figured I could do it," she says. "You don't need a college degree to do an honest day's work."

Why have so few entrepreneurs applied for the new program? For one thing, the approval process is arduous and
risky. Prospective Americans must first make the investment
plunge and then wait two years before the federal government will even consider issuing a permanent visa. The approval process itself can take up to a year. "If the business
fails before you get your final papers, you could get deported," says Howard Hom, a Los Angeles immigration
lawyer. Many entrepreneurs and investors with money to
spare have bypassed the United States and headed for
Canada. Little wonder. The red tape there is minimal, and
the investment threshold can be as low as $250,000. Result:
Canada has attracted some $3 billion in new investment
since 1986, far more than the United States is on track to
achieve.

Other than stealing a page from Canada, what else should
Washington do? Approving a few additional impact grants
to help cities that host the poorest of arrivals might make
sense. But footing local bills entirely is not the answer, since
these communities ultimately benefit from immigrants' economic activism. Instead, Washington ought to consider dou-
bling what it spends on English-language programs for

children and adults, to about $1 billion. Learning their adopted land's tongue, most immigrants agree, is the hardest challenge they face and the biggest barrier to getting a foot on the job ladder—and then climbing it.

Supporting efforts like the North American Free Trade Agreement should also help bolster Third World economies and stem the tide of impoverished, unskilled workers seeking opportunity in the United States. Certainly NAFTA seems a far better bet than trying to police 7,582 miles of border with fewer than 4,000 patrolmen. Economist Sherman Robinson of the University of California at Berkeley estimates that each percentage point increase in the value of Mexico's capital stock—the new buildings, businesses, and factories that a NAFTA-spurred investment boom would give rise to—would be enough stimulus to keep 35,000 of its citizens at home.

Finally, if Bill Clinton is really hankering for an exciting new way to shake up U.S. immigration policy and boost job creation, here's a terrific idea from Nobel Prize–winning economist Gary Becker: sell visas. Fix the price at perhaps $50,000 or some level sufficient to attract those seriously seeking opportunity, not a free ride. Lack of wealth or skills should not exclude prospective Americans. Let the poor come on a federal loan that they would have to pay back over time or face deportation. "This would ensure we would get only the ambitious," says Becker. What better population screen could the United States ask for?

Tired, Poor, on Welfare
George J. Borjas

George J. Borjas is professor of economics at the University of California, San Diego, and the author of *Friends or Strangers: The Impact of Immigrants on the U.S. Economy*. This essay is excerpted from "Tired, Poor, on Welfare," which first appeared in the *National Review*, December 13, 1993.

MORE IMMIGRANTS WILL enter the United States during the 1990s than in any other decade in the country's history. We are now admitting over 800,000 legal immigrants annually, and at least 200,000 illegal aliens manage to evade the Border Patrol and settle here permanently. It is not surprising, therefore, that immigration has become a charged political issue. Previous debates revolved around the questions of how well immigrants assimilate and whether they take jobs away from natives. The rapid growth of entitlement programs in the past three decades introduces an additional explosive question: do they pay their way in the welfare state?

• • •

In 1990 cash benefits received by immigrants totaled $4 billion. We do not know precisely the extent of immigrant participation in noncash programs (such as Medicaid and food stamps). However, if immigrants use these other programs to the same extent that they receive cash benefits, they would account for 13 percent of the cost of all means-tested entitlement programs, or about $24 billion. In 1990 immigrant households received a total income (net of welfare payments) of $285 billion. Recent estimates of the total tax burden faced by U.S. households at various income levels suggest that the average federal tax rate for the immigrant population is around 22 percent. Including state and local taxes would bring it up to around 30 percent, or around $85 billion.

Clearly, immigrants pay more in taxes ($85 billion) than they take out of the welfare system ($24 billion). But this comparison is completely irrelevant. It is, in effect, saying that immigrants' taxes are used only to fund cash welfare programs. One can justify this calculation by arguing that most other government programs provide "public goods," and that expenditures would be the same whether or not we had an immigrant population. However, a larger population will lead to more crowded freeways and parks, schools and hospitals, thus increasing the cost of providing these public goods. Immigrants obviously benefit from these programs and so should be assigned a user fee for them.

But what should we charge them? It should seem logical to charge immigrants their "fair share" of the costs of the various programs, so that if 21 percent of our taxes fund defense, then 21 percent of immigrant taxes should be allocated to defense expenditures. It turns out that only about 9 percent of our taxes fund means-tested entitlement programs, so that immigrants contribute $8 billion to their funding (9 percent of $85 billion). Comparing the $8 billion contribution with the $24 billion expenditure, immigrants impose a $16 billion annual burden on native taxpayers.

Now $16 billion is equivalent to a reduction in national income of 0.3 percent! Moreover, these net costs must be contrasted with the economic benefits. It is evident that employers (as well as consumers) benefit from the presence of a large pool of unskilled workers in the labor force. The available evidence, however, suggests that these benefits are also a tiny fraction of national income, again on the order of 0.2 or 0.3 percent. At the national level, therefore, it would not be farfetched to conclude that immigration is a near washout.

But these accounting exercises—though they make nice headlines—are beside the point. In the end, the true costs of immigrant participation in welfare programs have little, if anything, to do with the bottom line. Expenditures on the AFDC program, after all, total only about $22 billion annually. The raging debate over welfare in the past thirty years is not over $22 billion. Rather, it is over the possibility that welfare slowly saps a recipient's work incentives, encourages the breakdown of the family unit, and transmits welfare dependency across generations. These are the disturbing consequences that should worry observers of the immigrant experience.

There are some facts about immigrant participation in welfare programs that are striking and indisputable and that do not depend on assumptions about how much we should charge immigrants for public services they receive. In 1970 immigrants were slightly less likely than natives to receive cash benefits such as AFDC or SSI. By 1990 the situation had changed drastically: over 9 percent of immigrant households received public assistance, as opposed to about 7 percent of native households.

Not only are immigrants more likely to be on welfare, but they also get more benefits. The typical foreign-born welfare household received about $5,400 in cash benefits in 1990, as compared to $4,000 for a native household. As a result, even though immigrant households make up about 8 percent of the population, they account for 13 percent of the expenditures in cash-benefit programs.

This alarming increase has occurred partly because more recent immigrant waves are relatively less skilled than earlier waves. In 1960 the immigrants admitted into the country actually had more schooling than natives. By 1990 the new immigrants had far less schooling than natives, meaning they were likelier to earn low incomes, and therefore to qualify for many welfare programs.

Unfortunately, the debate has focused recently on welfare expenditures incurred by *illegal* aliens, and particularly by so-called citizen-children (the U.S.-born children of illegal aliens who are citizens and thus qualify for social services). Since one in four new cases on the California AFDC caseload is a citizen-child, it is no surprise that illegal aliens are at the center of the debate. Illegals, however, are only part of the problem. Over 12 percent of non-Mexican immigrant households in California receive public assistance. There are also frighteningly high rates of welfare dependency among refugee populations. Even after being in the country for five years, about two-thirds of Laotian and Cambodian households in California, as well as over one-third of Vietnamese households, receive public assistance. Immigrant households make up only 21 percent of California's population, but receive one-third of all cash benefits distributed in the state.

• • •

Immigrant-rights groups often dismiss these facts by claiming that immigrants come to the United States looking for jobs, not to get on the welfare rolls. That may well be true, but the point is simply irrelevant. Even immigrants who want to work find it hard to predict what they will actually encounter when they enter the U.S. labor market. Many immigrants are probably dismayed to find that the roads in Los Angeles and New York are not paved with gold, and that the types of jobs available and the incomes that their skills can command are far below what they expected. As it happens, immigrants are *more* likely to receive welfare benefits the longer they reside in the United States. It seems that assimilation involves learning not only about labor-market opportunities, but also about the programs that make up the welfare state.

Regardless of whether the bottom line on the immigration ledger sheet is minus $2 billion or minus $20 billion, the facts are alarming enough. Because of the increasing proportion of the unskilled among those who reach our shores (or who run across the border), more and more immigrants land on the welfare rolls, even if this was not the driving force of their migration. The potential already exists for the creation of a large new underclass of workers in our society, composed mainly of less skilled immigrants, who will be accorded all the dysfunctional benefits of government assistance. The policy implication is clear: a welfare state cannot afford the large-scale immigration of less-skilled persons.

Illegal Immigration:
Would a National ID Card Help?
Robert Kuttner

Robert Kuttner is economics correspondent for the *New Republic* and the author of *The End of Laissez-Faire.* "Illegal Immigration: Would a National ID Card Help?" first appeared in *Business Week,* August 26, 1991.

PEEK INTO ANY U.S. hotel or restaurant kitchen, and you are likely to spy foreigners without green cards through the dishwater steam. These workers are known as "illegal aliens" or more benignly as "undocumented workers," depending on your view of the issue. Foreigners unauthorized to work in the United States can also be found in garment factories, tomato fields, parking garages, taxi cabs, behind a broom, and performing a host of other tasks whose common features are long hours, scut work, and low pay. Millions of such workers continue to flood the labor force, despite a long-fought 1986 immigration-reform law that liberalized legal immigration in exchange for what was supposed to be a crackdown on unlawful entry and employment.

The novel idea of the 1986 law was to hold businesses accountable for hiring improperly documented workers. But the law had to be watered down to win enactment because of opposition from employers, who justifiably resisted being deputized as border guards, and from civil rights groups with legitimate fears that anyone with a Hispanic surname or Asian features might be subjected to the third degree. In practice, an employer need only make a reasonable effort to examine a worker's documents—a Social Security card will usually do—and the employer is legally off the hook. But of course, such documents are notoriously easy to forge or misuse.

Long Hours.

In the real world, according to a source in the restaurant industry, the system works like this: An unauthorized immigrant job applicant produces either a borrowed Social Security card or a forged one. Other corroborating fake IDs are even easier to get. The worker then claims a very large family—so many that no withholding is taken out of his or her paycheck. My source says he doesn't know—or care—which of his employees are working under their own names, which ones are citizens, or which ones are aliens. What he does know, he says, is that they are all hard workers. Many of them work the breakfast shift at one restaurant, the day shift at another, and even dinner at a third. Living collectively and working a fourteen- or sixteen-hour day, they can make close to $1,000 a week effectively tax-free except for deductions for FICA (Federal Insurance Contribution Act). Most of their earnings are sent home to El Salvador or Colombia. Or Nigeria, or Ireland, or China, or Haiti, or Mexico, or wherever.

What are we to make of this? In a sense, there is a crude social bargain here. The unauthorized workers enjoy the benefits of U.S. residence without paying U.S. income tax. U.S. consumers and employers get the benefits of these hard-working foreigners, whose wages—though low—are infinitely greater than they could earn in their homelands.

On the other hand, foreigners receive no benefits from payroll deductions credited to bogus Social Security numbers. Also, billions of dollars' worth of wages are sent out of our economy, rather than going to purchase goods and services here. And hard-won benefits to American workers—minimum wage, the eight-hour day, pensions—are undermined by the enormous underground economy.

Ambivalence.

Recently, the Immigration and Naturalization Service announced the latest in a series of futile crackdowns. Between May and August of this year [1991], approximately $3.2 million in fines were imposed on employers for hiring obvious illegals. But that's about a dollar for each of the estimated two million to four million foreigners working illegally in the United States. For the entire country, the INS has only about 1,800 special agents working in nonborder areas. with several hundred of them devoting their time to other matters, such as smuggling or fake marriages.

The deeper problem, I suspect, is a profound public ambivalence about the entire question. With the exception of Native Americans, we are a nation of immigrants. Some of our parents and grandparents sneaked into this country and went on not only to thrive but to give a good deal back. In the 1960s, when liberals were indignant about illegal migrant workers, conservatives responded that such workers were more of an asset than a drain on the economy. That debate continues. Some have even argued that our borders should simply be thrown open.

Moreover, Americans also have a pathological distrust of government identification cards. Until recently Social Security cards included the utterly disingenuous disclaimer "For Social Security and tax purposes—not for identification," even though Social Security numbers are now in standard use for driver's licenses, bank accounts, insurance policies, passport applications, and so on.

If America were more adult about this issue, like some Western European nations, we might save ourselves endless inconvenience by establishing a single official ID. Employers could ask to see it, and counterfeiting it would be a serious crime.

That way, Americans might finally decide just what sort of immigration policy they really want and have that policy enforced. The current situation, while randomly helping a number of lucky individual migrant workers, has the corrosive side effect of eroding the rule of law.

Aging America
Needs Foreign Blood
Peter Francese

Peter Francese is president of *American Demographics Magazine* and author of *Capturing Customers*. "Aging America Needs Foreign Blood" originally appeared in the *Wall Street Journal*, March 27, 1990.

THERE ARE POWERFUL demographic forces at work in the United States that virtually mandate federal policy be changed to permit more immigration than we have now. The rapid increase in the number of very elderly people, combined with declining numbers of young adults and a record low population growth rate, will put this nation in a demographic vise.

Paying for the income security and medical needs of the elderly while at the same time improving the educational opportunities and well-being of children (not to mention paying interest on the federal deficit and rebuilding infrastructure) will squeeze future U.S. workers in the grip of higher federal payroll taxes, state taxes, and local property taxes. This is not just some distant problem beginning when the huge baby boom starts retiring in twenty years. The vise is closing now, particularly in the slow-growing Northeast and Midwest regions.

Overall U.S. population growth for the 1990s is projected to be only about 7 percent, a record low. The previous low was 7.2 percent growth during the Depression years of the

1930s. But almost all states in the Northeast and Midwest are expected to have growth rates below even that meager average. Regional population projections done by the Census Bureau using recent interstate migration trends show a continuing outflow of people from the Northeast and Midwest, resulting in growth rates for the 1990s of less than 2 percent. According to one scenario, four states in those regions could lose a combined total of nearly half a million people in the next ten years.

A state or region without any population growth loses on three fronts.

First, it loses political representation and therefore political power. The Northeast, for example, which lost nine congressional representatives after the 1960 census, is projected to lose an additional six following the 1990 census. This is on top of nine lost after the 1980 census. Loss of population can also result in less federal aid, because population size is frequently included in grant formulas.

Second, no-growth areas in the United States age more rapidly than those that are growing, thus driving up health-care expenditures. Pennsylvania, for example, which could lose more than 100,000 residents in the next ten years, is the second-oldest state in the nation, with half its population over age thirty-five versus the national median age of thirty-three. Within fifteen years half of the state's residents are expected to be more than forty years old. As a result, Pennsylvania will be one of the first states to experience more deaths than births, perpetuating its population decline.

Third, areas in the United States with no growth or a decline in population will experience more severe labor shortages in the years ahead, which tends to discourage new business investments. Labor shortages will be exacerbated by the shrinking population of young adults. Nationally, the number of people aged twenty to twenty-nine is projected by the Census Bureau to drop 12 percent in the next decade.

But in the Northeast and Midwest regions, the number is projected to shrink even more.

Employers or governments in regions with little or no growth could relieve labor shortages if they could recruit freely from abroad. Or they could reverse their population decline and offset the aging effect if they could encourage young adults to emigrate from other countries. But they can't, because while money and goods flow quite freely across our borders, workers do not. People from other countries can buy all the U.S. property or corporations they can afford, but they can't come to work here except in very small numbers.

Lack of population growth is a phenomenon specific to certain regions or states, but rapid growth of the very elderly and the need to improve educational opportunities for our children are national in scope. During the 1990s, for example, the number of people aged eighty-five and older is projected by the Census Bureau to grow 42 percent, six times the rate of overall population growth. This is on top of a 44 percent increase during the 1980s, when the overall population grew only 10 percent.

The medical needs of this population are enormous. A majority suffer from one or more chronic conditions and one-fifth are in long-term-care facilities. The nursing-home requirement alone means creating seventy-five to one hundred nursing-home beds every day for at least the next twenty years. If the cost of a stay in a nursing home averages only $100 per day during the 1990s, providing such care for the additional people aged eighty-five and older will add at least a billion dollars a year to our national health-care bill. But every two to three nursing-home beds requires an additional health-care worker. The worsening shortage of health-care workers will make this problem even more complex and expensive.

At the other end of the age scale, the school-age population is projected to grow 7 percent during the 1990s, the same rate as the overall population. This would seem to be a manageable growth rate in ordinary circumstances. But these are not ordinary times. U.S. schools need to be brought up to the standards of our overseas competitors, whose students spend more hours a day in school and attend more days per year. At the same time we need to compensate for the serious problem that one-fifth of U.S. schoolchildren live in poverty. Learning under those circumstances is more difficult and requires more support staffers.

Caring for our elderly and creating a brighter future for our children will certainly require a lot more money, but it will also require more people to teach and to care. Neither of those functions lends itself to automation.

By continuing to restrict immigration tightly we shoot ourselves in both feet. In the short run, our productive capacity is crippled by worker shortages, and in the long run, we will be hobbled by high dependency ratios—too many elderly dependents for too few workers.

Restrictive U.S. immigration laws are not just our problem, either. The weak economies of Latin America cannot possibly create jobs rapidly enough to absorb the additional fourteen million young adults (aged twenty to twenty-nine) expected there between 1990 and 2000. Many of those unable to find enough work to sustain themselves and their families will either come here illegally or worsen the already serious problem of political instability in Latin America. Increased illegal immigration breeds disrespect for a law that cannot be enforced. Stopping the flow of illegal immigration from Latin America may become a law-enforcement quagmire like trying to stop the flow of illegal drugs.

Tens of millions of legal immigrants and their descendants have contributed their imagination and vitality to the building of this nation. Future immigrants can contribute greatly to its rebuilding, because most immigrants are young and pay much more in taxes than they use in public services. Thus they can ease the squeeze future U.S. workers will feel as our slow-growing population ages.

We cannot wait twenty years to see what will happen when the baby boomers retire and ask what happened to their Social Security trust fund. The United States needs to admit more immigrants now to get us out of the demographic bind we put ourselves in by restricting immigration in the first place.

Immigration and the Environment
Nick Ervin

Nick Ervin is the conservation chairperson of the San Diego Sierra Club. His writing has appeared in the *San Diego Union Tribune* and *High Sierran.* "Immigration and the Environment" originally appeared under the title "Facing the Immigration Issue" in *Wild Earth,* Summer 1993.

IN LATE 1991 the United Nations released its first major report on overpopulation and its link to the disastrous deterioration of our global commons. Population biologists like Drs. Paul and Anne Ehrlich often speak in terms of the equation I = PAT, or Impact = Population x Affluence x Technology. Otherwise stated, humanity's impact on the biosphere equals the cumulative effects of (1) the size of the human population, (2) the level of affluence (amount of resource consumption), and (3) the technology utilized. Within this equation lies the key to why the developed nations pose the gravest threat to the systems supporting all life.

Although we in the United States make up less than 5 percent of the world human family, we consume an estimated 30 percent of world resources. The rate of consumption more than compensates for a population density and growth rate lower than in much of the developing world.

Our nation's and world's carrying capacities have been exceeded. Put differently, populations are already damaging planetary life-support systems (fresh water, clean air, fertile topsoil, and accessible minerals). We Americans maintain our lavish lifestyles only by importing massive quantities of energy resources (e.g., oil) and by extracting our own natural materials at unsustainable levels (mining, overgrazing, excessive timber cutting, overcropping to soil exhaustion, and oil and gas extraction).

One sensitive component of the population issue domestically is immigration. The major national conservation organizations have tiptoed genteelly around the issue, fearing adverse political repercussions. A few more specialized groups, particularly Negative Population Growth, and Population-Environment Balance, have courageously broached the topic with specific proposals. Unfortunately the Reagan government during the 1980s gutted many family-planning programs at home and abroad. Under George Bush we took several more steps backward, most notably modification of immigration policy, making it easier for foreigners with relatives already living here to immigrate. It has been estimated that the backlog overseas of those qualifying under the new rules approaches twenty million. These changes were enacted at the same time a scientifically conducted random poll by the Roper Organization found that 87 percent of Americans believe the United States has a population problem. Of those, two-thirds supported reducing legal immigration and better than nine in ten supported an "all-out" effort to stop illegal immigration.

The 1991 United Nations report on population and the environment persuasively laid out the scientific evidence linking human population and consumption patterns and the ongoing ruination of our biosphere. The effects of such deterioration in terms of real human suffering alone—starvation, economic exploitation, and crime—are becoming starkly apparent. Meanwhile, the United States increases its human population by three million per year, of which 1.2 to 1.9 million, depending on your source, are immigrants, legal and illegal. America has the highest fertility rate of any developed nation on earth and we permit more legal immigrants through our borders than the rest of the world combined—up to one million per year when all classes are included in the numbers: refugees, those under regular formulas, and people with family members already residing here (who are not included in the restricted quota numbers).

California absorbs fully one-third of total U.S. immigration and, partly as a result, tops the country in its fertility rate of 2.48 children per couple (1989). U.S. Census Bureau figures released in 1992 showed that one San Diego resident in five was born in a foreign land.

Considerable media attention is devoted to the social and financial costs associated with such statistics. We hear about increasingly crowded school classrooms, overburdened hospital emergency rooms, and packed local justice systems.

The largely untold story revolves around the ramifications for America's natural areas and environment quality, which are badly strained by the growing numbers of human beings here, including immigrants. Some examples: between 1984 and 1990 California lost 140,000 acres of prime agricultural land to development; only 5 percent of this country's original virgin forests remain uncut, as largely population-induced demand for wood products soars; up to two-thirds of our Western rangelands are in unsatisfactory condition due to overgrazing by domestic livestock raised, ostensibly, to feed and clothe our people; natural aquifers are being drained to slake our population's thirst for water and demand for irrigated food crops.

Moreover, immigration into the United States means higher consumption rates globally and higher fertility rates nationally. Anne and Paul Ehrlich explain: ". . . from a global environment perspective, immigration into the United States is not neutral . . . even the less well-off [immigrants] quickly acquire American superconsuming habits. They tend to bring with them the reproductive habits of their societies, so that they also produce larger families of superconsumers than those of us whose families immigrated earlier."

Some in the conservation community are working to alter the established policies of the major national conservation groups in favor of aggressive and specific stands on immigration. In part these advocates propose we embrace a policy known as "no net increase" with respect to legal immigrants which permits only the same number of legal immigrants into this country each year as the number of American residents who leave permanently—about 200,000. No position is taken on whom should be allowed in, just the overall number. Further public discussion would establish priorities.

Of course, legal immigration is only part of a larger picture. In order to stabilize and then reduce totally U.S. population, we will need to take additional measures to curb illegal entry, offer more family-planning resources to developing nations, and adopt our own comprehensive domestic blueprint for stabilization and reduction. Such measures will, perforce, require an extraordinary public debate in our country on such touchy topics as contraceptive availability, family-planning education in the schools, tax code disincentives for large-family creation, and control of our international borders. This debate will be ethically complex and politically difficult. We must face it squarely.

Authentic immigration reform proposals with teeth in them will almost certainly draw intense fire. Proponents have been and will again be accused of racism, elitism, or at least a chilly lack of compassion for the less fortunate. Edward Abbey, for one, drew vitriolic condemnation from many quarters in the 1980s for his prickly opinions on immigration. I firmly believe, nonetheless, that we do neither our homeland nor our planet (including its human members) a favor by acting as a continuing sponge for immigrants from other lands. In doing so, we retard the impetus behind population and economic reforms in other nations while seriously reducing the present and future basis for taking care of those who live here now, including recent immigrants. Large numbers of immigrants now enter an America ill-equipped to house or employ them adequately. They too often join an exploited, permanent underclass trapped in poverty and joblessness or underemployment.

Growth in America, as elsewhere in this finite world, cannot continue indefinitely; one way or another population growth and runaway consumption will be halted. The longer we delay in taking aggressive, tenacious actions, the more draconian the ultimate solutions will be (ever hear of the Four Horsemen of the Apocalypse?).

The Clinton administration has taken some promising initial steps on population. The President has reversed the Reagan-Bush stance on support for the UN Fund for Population Activities and overseas agencies providing abortion counseling among their family-planning services. While helpful, these actions were simple compared to what lies ahead. The United States still lags far behind the funding targets it accepted in 1989 for overseas family-planning services—the "Amsterdam Declaration" goal of providing contraceptives to all couples worldwide who wish them by the year 2000. And one can only imagine the level of opposition by the "wise use" crowd and its religious-right allies to real government-sponsored incentives for small families; genuine access for all classes of people to therapeutic abortions and contraceptives; widespread and biocentric family/sex education in the schools; or significant increases in money earmarked for population control overseas.

As conscious, aware beings we must take concrete action now to ensure human numbers no larger than what can be sustained at decent material standards over the indefinite future without destroying our fellow living creatures. To fail in this effort insults all races and classes of our citizenry. It also betrays the trust of our descendants who inherit the Earth we have borrowed from them.

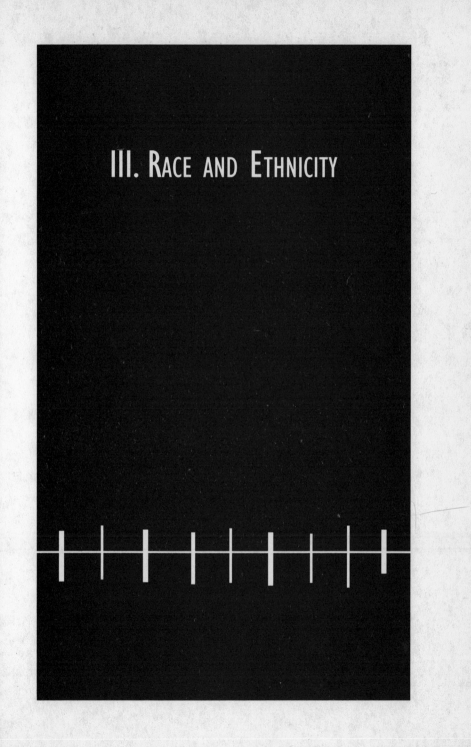

III. Race and Ethnicity

On the Backs of Blacks
Toni Morrison

Toni Morrison is the 1993 winner of the Nobel Prize
for Literature and Robert F. Goheen Professor, Council
of the Humanities, Princeton University. Her novels include *Sula, Song of Solomon,* and *Beloved,* which won the
1988 Pulitzer Prize for Fiction. "On the Backs of Blacks"
first appeared in *Time* in 1993.

FRESH FROM ELLIS Island, Stavros gets a job shining shoes at Grand Central Terminal. It is the last scene of
Elia Kazan's film *America, America,* the story of a young
Greek's fierce determination to immigrate to America.
Quickly, but as casually as an afterthought, a young black
man, also a shoe shiner, enters and tries to solicit a cus-
tomer. He is run off the screen—"Get out of here! We're doing business here!"—and silently disappears.

This interloper into Stavros's workplace is crucial in the
mix of signs that make up the movie's happy-ending immigrant story: a job, a straw hat, an infectious smile—and a
scorned black. It is the act of racial contempt that trans-
forms this charming Greek into an entitled white. Without
it, Stavros's future as an American is not at all assured.

This is race talk, the explicit insertion into everyday life of
racial signs and symbols that have no meaning other than
pressing African Americans to the lowest level of the racial
hierarchy. Popular culture, shaped by film, theater, advertis-
ing, the press, television, and literature, is heavily engaged

in race talk. It participates freely in this most enduring and efficient rite of passage into American culture: negative appraisals of the native-born black population. Only when the lesson of racial estrangement is learned is assimilation complete. Whatever the lived experience of immigrants with African Americans—pleasant, beneficial, or bruising—the rhetorical experience renders blacks as noncitizens, already discredited outlaws.

All immigrants fight for jobs and space, and who is there to fight but those who have both? As in the fishing ground struggle between Texas and Vietnamese shrimpers, they displace what and whom they can. Although U.S. history is awash in labor battles, political fights, and property wars among all religious and ethnic groups, their struggles are persistently framed as struggles between recent arrivals and blacks. In race talk the move into mainstream America always means buying into the notion of American blacks as the real aliens. Whatever the ethnicity or nationality of the immigrant, his nemesis is understood to be African American.

Current attention to immigration has reached levels of panic not seen since the turn of the century. To whip up this panic, modern race talk must be revised downward into obscurity and nonsense if antiblack hostility is to remain the drug of choice, giving headlines their kick. PATTERNS OF IMMIGRATION FOLLOWED BY WHITE FLIGHT, screams the *Star-Ledger* in Newark. The message we are meant to get is that disorderly newcomers are dangerous to stable (white) residents. Stability is white. Disorder is black. Nowhere do we learn what stable middle-class blacks think or do to cope with the "breaking waves of immigration." The overwhelming majority of African Americans, hardworking and stable, are out of the loop, have disappeared except in their less-than-covert function of defining whites as the "true" Americans.

So addictive is this ploy that the fact of blackness has been abandoned for the theory of blackness. It doesn't matter anymore what shade the newcomer's skin is. A hostile posture toward resident blacks must be struck at the Americanizing door before it will open. The public is asked to accept American blacks as the common denominator in each conflict between an immigrant and a job or between a wannabe and status. It hardly matters what complexities, contexts, and misinformation accompany these conflicts. They can all be subsumed as the equation of brand X versus blacks.

But more than a job is at stake in this surrender to whiteness, more even than what the black intellectual W. E. B. Du Bois called the "psychological wage"—the bonus of whiteness. Racist strategies unify. Savvy politicians always include in the opening salvos of their campaigns a quick clarification of their position on race. It is a mistake to think that Bush's Willie Horton or Clinton's Sister Souljah was anything but a candidate's obligatory response to the demands of a contentious electorate unable to understand itself in any terms other than race. Warring interests, nationalities, and classes can be merged with the greatest economy under that racial banner.

Race talk as bonding mechanism is powerfully on display in American literature. When Nick in F. Scott Fitzgerald's *The Great Gatsby* leaves West Egg to dine in fashionable East Egg, his host conducts a kind of class audition into WASP-dom by soliciting Nick's support for the "science" of racism. "If we don't look out the white race will be . . . utterly submerged," he says. "It's all scientific stuff; it's been proved." It makes Nick uneasy, but he does not question or refute his host's convictions.

The best clue to what the country might be like without race as the nail upon which American identity is hung comes from Pap, in Mark Twain's *Huckleberry Finn,* who upon learning a Negro could vote in Ohio, "drawed out. I says I'll never vote ag'in." Without his glowing white mask he is not American; he is Faulkner's character Wash, in *Absalom, Absalom!* who, stripped of the mask and treated like a "nigger," drives a scythe into the heart of the rich white man he has loved and served so completely.

For Pap, for Wash, the possibility that race talk might signify nothing was frightening. Which may be why the harder it is to speak race talk convincingly, the more people seem to need it. As American blacks occupy more and more groups no longer formed along racial lines, the pressure accelerates to figure out what white interests really are. The enlisted military is almost one-quarter black; police forces are blackening in large urban areas. But welfare is nearly two-thirds white; affirmative-action beneficiaries are overwhelmingly white women; dysfunctional white families jam the talk shows and court TV.

The old stereotypes fail to connote, and race talk is forced to invent new, increasingly mindless ones. There is virtually no movement up—for blacks or whites, established classes or arrivistes—that is not accompanied by race talk. Refusing, negotiating, or fulfilling this demand is the real stuff, the organizing principle of becoming an American. Star-spangled. Race-strangled.

Blacks vs. Browns
Jack Miles

Jack Miles is a member of the editorial board of the *Los Angeles Times* and the director of that newspaper's literary awards program. "Blacks vs. Browns" first appeared in the *Atlantic Monthly,* October 1992.

DURING THE 1980s, according to census figures released in May 1992, the United States admitted 8.6 million immigrants. In the context of U.S. immigration history this is a staggering number—more than in any decade since 1900–10. Worldwide, half the decade's emigrants had made the United States their destination. Of them, 11 percent—more than three-quarters of a million—further specified their choice as Los Angeles. By the end of the decade 40 percent of all Angelenos were foreign-born; 49.9 percent spoke a language other than English at home; 25.3 percent spoke Spanish. This is the city where, two weeks before those figures were released, the most violent urban riot in American history broke out: fifty-one people were killed, and property worth $750 million or more was lost.

Though the occasion for the riot was the acquittal of four white policemen on charges of assaulting a black traffic offender, Latinos as well as African Americans rioted. Why? What was Rodney King to Latinos? Did a race riot, once begun, degenerate—or progress—into a bread riot? Was it a vast crime spree, as devoid of political content as the looting that followed the 1977 blackout in New York City? Of those

arrested afterward—of whom more than half were Latino—
40 percent already had criminal records. Was the riot a de-
feat of the police? If it was a hybrid of all these, was it,
finally, an aberration from which, by hard work, America's
second-largest city could recover? Or was it the annuncia-
tion of a new and permanent state of affairs?

I work at the *Los Angeles Times,* writing a column for that
newspaper's book supplement and unsigned editorials three
or four times a week for its editorial page. On the day after
the first night of the riot, one of my colleagues said to me, as
we left to hunt for a still-open restaurant, "When the bar-
barians sacked Rome in 410, the Romans thought it was the
end of civilization. You smile—but what followed was the
Dark Ages." Think of what follows here as the voice of a
worried Roman—in front of a television set, watching the
Goths at their sack.

Meeting Latino Los Angeles

I came to Los Angeles in 1978, to work as an editor in the
branch office of the University of California Press at UCLA.
The first home I owned here was a house trailer in Malibu.
In 1981 a Santa Ana—one of the notorious local wind-
storms—ripped off the carport attached to the trailer and
did some further damage to the roof. My wife and I had
some insurance, but not enough. To help me complete my
do-it-yourself repairs, I hired two Mexican boys from the
pool of laborers who gathered daily near a shopping center
just off the Pacific Coast Highway. One of the two, Ricky
Rodríguez (not his real name), just fifteen years old when we
met him, would become almost literally a member of our
family.

One Sunday afternoon, after Ricky had been working
with me part-time for several weeks, a Coast Highway land-
slide cut Malibu in half, and we invited Ricky to stay

overnight. The buses weren't running. His alternatives, both illegal, were sleeping on the beach and sleeping in some neglected patch of brush along the road. He accepted the invitation and on the morrow brought my wife and me a breakfast in bed consisting of fried eggs and peanut butter sandwiches. In the sudden, unforeseen intimacy of the moment, a kind of conversation began different from any we had yet had. We began to learn something about his family.

Ricky, his mother, two sisters, and a brother were living in City Terrace Park, a neighborhood in East Los Angeles, as the permanent houseguests of another sister, her husband, and their two small children: nine people in a two-bedroom cottage. Ricky's brother-in-law, at the time the only American citizen in the family, was a cook whose generous employer had bought him his cottage. (Later, Juan José—called Juanjo for short—would open his own burrito shop.) Ricky invited me to visit his family, and I did so. I had never been in the barrio before.

Ricky continued working for us over several months. Relations remained friendly, and he eventually asked if we would adopt him, purely for legal reasons: to make him a citizen. His mother and I visited a sympathetic Chicano immigration lawyer, but Mexico's laws protecting its children made the move legally complicated. I did agree, however, to tutor Ricky through his remaining two years of high school—and here we return to the riot as an event in a mecca for immigrants.

As a taxpayer, I was surprised—not that I wasn't happy for our young friend—to discover that his status as an illegal immigrant was no bar to his attending high school at state expense. He did have to show a birth certificate; but, interestingly, his mother, a short, stout, indomitably cheerful woman who had crossed the border as a single mother with four children, of whom the youngest was a toddler at the time, had brought birth certificates with her. She had had education on her mind from the start, and a Guadalajara certificate was certificate enough for Wilson High School, which received money from the state on a per-capita basis and would have lost money had illegal immigrants been denied admission.

Another surprise came in Ricky's senior year, when he asked if I would accompany him to the Department of Motor Vehicles and permit him to take a driving test in my car. (My presence and signature may have been required in some other capacity as well; I can no longer quite remember.) I knew by then that illegal immigrants commonly drove the streets and freeways of Los Angeles without any kind of driver's license. Ricky wanted a license mainly because it provided an identification card and a degree of cover for someone seeking work. He took and passed the test in the Lincoln Heights DMV office not far from downtown Los Angeles.

But here again I was surprised that no proof of legal residency was requested for the receipt of a California driver's license. On the Coast Highway, I had witnessed hair-raising "sweeps" by Immigration and Naturalization Service agents on the very corner where I had hired Ricky. Such chases farther south, at an INS checkpoint on Interstate 5, north of San Diego, led with grim frequency to traffic deaths. Why did the INS not simply come to the DMV office in Lincoln Heights and arrest applicants? As we waited in line to deliver Ricky's completed written test, we overheard the clerk administering the same test orally—in Spanish—to a short older man with a copper Amerindian face. He would have fallen one answer short of the passing grade had she not given him a broad hint.

The DMV office had as foreign a feel to it as the *correro* in Mexico City. One heard almost no English at all. Ricky took his test not long after Election Day that year. The contrast between the two populations—the one in the polling station, the other at the DMV—was overwhelming. The DMV office seemed to be a part of the American administration of some foreign—or indigenous but subject—population.

A Latino Riot?

Back to the riot: was there a political motive for the Latino rioting? There is a radical fringe of Chicano activists with a political agenda for the land they call Azlán: northwest Mexico and the southwest United States. They claim, not without reason, that Chicano farmworkers now sweat on land stolen from their ancestors. But Ricky and his family take a different view. I learned in passing that as an eighth-grader Ricky had donned a feather headdress and a loin-cloth and danced in a "folkloric" group organized by one of his teachers, but the Aztecs meant no more to him than the Illinois did to me as a Boy Scout in Chicago. Ricky's older brother, Victor, once asked me in puzzlement why Americans gave Spanish names to their houses and boats. Why not English names? A rich and interesting question, perhaps, but not one that betrayed a political agenda.

We learned later that in fact many if not most of the Latino rioters were either Central Americans or very recent Mexican immigrants, and that what the riot might have been to us Anglos, it was also, to some considerable extent, to the established Mexican-American political leadership. They, too, were wondering about a huge, strange, possibly angry, Spanish-speaking population in their midst. Who were these people, and what did they want? If they had no political agenda, if they were common criminals, well, that, too—given their growing numbers and the demonstrated inadequacy of the police—was news, wasn't it? The population of South Central Los Angeles had doubled since 1965. For every black in the area there was now at least one Latino. That had to make a difference. But what kind of difference?

In the weeks following the riot, Latino leaders from East Los Angeles were concerned that the sudden spotlight on South Central Los Angeles would rob them of scarce government funds. They were on guard against the possibility that South Central Los Angeles would be rewarded for its violence and East Los Angeles punished for its good behavior. "Just because we didn't erupt in East L.A., does that translate into us being ignored or missing out on the funds that are funneling into the communities?" asked Geraldine Zapata, the executive director of the Plaza Community Center. But the more immediate challenge to Mexican East Los Angeles was coming to terms with Central American South Central Los Angeles.

The Watts II Paradigm: Blacks vs. Whites

The mainstream interpretation had little to say about either Mexicans or Central Americans. It took the riot to be Watts II, a repetition of the 1965 black riot, touched off by the verdict in the King case but growing out of the deeper frustrations of the black population over rising unemployment, institutionalized police brutality, and eroded public assistance. That interpretation was surely right as far as it went. Those who mentally bracketed the riot between the videotaped beatings of King by a gang of white policemen and of Reginald Denny, a white trucker, by a gang of black rioters were not altogether wrong to do so.

And this interpretation was reinforced during the weeks following the riot by the competing rhetoric of black rappers on the one hand and the police on the other. On June 26, Police Chief Daryl F. Gates's last day on the job, Amnesty International released a report, "Police Brutality in Los Angeles," claiming that the department used its Taser guns and turned loose its dogs on suspects who were not resisting arrest or had already been taken into custody. LAPD brutality, the report claimed, "has even amounted to torture." Gates replied by denouncing the organization as "a bunch of knucklehead liberals" who "attack everything that is good in the country . . . and good in the world."

Earlier, Sergeant Stacey C. Koon, the commanding officer in the King beating, had discussed his unpublished memoir, "The Ides of March," with reporters, apparently in an attempt to sell it. The manuscript includes the following description of Koon's treatment of a Latino said to be under the influence of the drug PCP (the same was said, wrongly, of Rodney King):

My boot came from the area of lower California and connected with the suspect's scrotum about lower Missouri. My boot stopped about Ohio, but the suspect's testicles continued into upper Maine. The suspect was literally lifted off the ground. The suspect tried to speak, but appeared he had something in his throat—probably his balls.

That beating, captured on videotape, became a popular training tool for young officers. "The tape was to become a legend in its own time," Koon wrote. A Latino may thus have been Koon's most abused victim. However, it was Koon's reference to King as "Mandingo" that attracted the most outraged comment. In general, the more post-riot analysis concentrated on violence and the police, the closer it stayed to the Watts II, black-white interpretation.

The same interpretation, though with one important qualification, was fostered by the popularity—among whites as well as blacks—of virulently racist, grotesquely violent black music, much of it originating in Los Angeles. On June 23 both the City Council and the County Board of Supervisors called on Time Warner and local retailers to discontinue sales of Ice-T's album *Body Count*. Later Willie L. Williams, the newly sworn-in black police chief, did the same. "Cop Killer," then one of the cuts on that album, includes the chorus:

COP KILLER, *it's better you than me.*
COP KILLER, *fuck police brutality!*
COP KILLER, *I know your family's grievin'*
(FUCK 'EM!)
COP KILLER, *but tonight we get even.*

Ice-T defended himself rather in the manner of a novelist. He told a New York audience, "At no point do I go out and say, 'Let's do it.' I'm singing in the first person as a character who is fed up with police brutality. I ain't never killed no cop. I felt like it a lot of times. But I never did it." This justification was a little thin for the grieving widow and daughter ("Fuck 'em!") of a slain officer who had testified before the City Council. Norma Williams's husband, Tom, was murdered by Daniel Jenkins, against whom he had testified in an armed-robbery case. Jenkins ambushed Williams as the policeman was picking up his six-year-old son at a day-care center, pumping eight bullets into the detective's body while the boy watched and later, according to the testimony of an accomplice, describing with pleasure how the victim's body convulsed with the impact of each bullet. "Cop Killer" has a spoken, prose prologue:

This next record is dedicated to some personal friends of mine, the LAPD. For every cop that has ever taken advantage of somebody, beat 'em down or hurt 'em, because they got long hair, listen to the wrong kind of music, the wrong color, whatever they thought was the reason to do it, for every one of those fuckin' police, I'd like to take a pig out here in this parkin' lot and shoot 'em in their motherfuckin' face.

Willie Williams's reaction to this was "I have major problems with it as an American, as a parent, and as a police officer. I have buried five police officers during my career. . . . I think it's a disgrace that any singer would use such vulgarity and give the implication that killing an officer is okay." Williams was joined by relatives of the slain officer as he called on Time Warner to withdraw the album: "I think that, minding the Constitution, it should be voluntarily withdrawn." Los Angeles's African-American Peace Officers' Association disagreed with the new chief, but on balance the "Cop Killer" controversy had kept the focus on blacks and the police and away from more complex, multi-ethnic readings of the riot.

As a riot paradigm, Watts II had two versions: the black and the white, or (almost, but not quite, the same) the liberal and the conservative. An independent commission, chaired by former Deputy Secretary of State Warren Christopher, had investigated the LAPD after the Rodney King beating and recommended major changes. The most important of them—limiting the chief's tenure in office and making him and the police department more clearly subordinate to elected government than they had been under the civil service model—were overwhelmingly approved by the voters in June. Liberals saw the future in that vote. Conservatives saw the future less in the vote than in the 64 percent jump in handgun purchases that followed the riot.

Welcoming the Troops

There is in fact more convergence here than meets the eye. Proposition F, the police-reform measure, passed despite fierce opposition by the chief and much of the police department, but it didn't pass because the voters wanted less policing. The LAPD has been a quasi-military, cold, hard, swift, but—most important—small and low-cost police force. The police have been in effect the domestic marines, flying in to put down insurrections. They have not been an occupying force, and yet an occupying force is precisely what the population wants and needs.

"Community policing," the alternative whose revival (there's nothing new about it) was urged by the Christopher Commission, amounts to a steady, low-level involvement by a resident force with the law-abiding portion of the population in the interests of more effectively controlling the law-breaking portion. During the riot the National Guard, which came and went in a matter of days, was far more like a community police force than the community's own police force. The news photographs—of Guardsmen talking to children, strolling in pairs down the sidewalks, and so forth—were of scenes that would be noticeably out of character for the hard-assed LAPD. An English friend of mine who a few years ago approached an LAPD officer in downtown Los Angeles to ask for directions was told "Buy a map." Whatever Los Angeles cops are, they are not helpful bobbies. "Smoked Pork," the opening cut on *Body Count,* begins with a playlet. A young black approaches a cop asking for help with a flat tire. The cop snaps, "No! That's not my job! My job is not to help your fuckin' ass out!" The black then "smokes" him.

The Guardsmen seemed young, small, out of shape, and amateurish by comparison with the LAPD, but the sentiment universally expressed when their withdrawal was announced was the wish that they would stay longer. Since the LAPD had failed to stop the outbreak of the riot, few had much confidence that it could stop a recurrence. More than that, there was a faint sense that the Guard had arrived not to reinforce the LAPD but as a peacekeeping force placed between the out-of-control citizenry and its out-of-control police force.

An Austrian-born editor of my acquaintance says that the way New Yorkers cope with street crime reminds him of the way ordinary Europeans navigated between the Nazis and the Resistance under Nazi occupation. The Resistance saw every citizen not known to be a partisan as potentially a collaborator, and therefore an enemy. The Nazis saw every ordinary citizen not known to be a collaborator as potentially a partisan, and therefore an enemy. In New York, my friend says, street criminals and the police, for different reasons, both look on ordinary citizens as potentially the enemy. Life for the ordinary citizen becomes, as a result, an endless round of precautions. One is never not on guard.

This comparison gives a paradoxical, probably unwelcome, confirmation to the black leaders who insisted on calling the Rodney King riot an "uprising." Though triggered by an action of the government, the riot had no real political content. The largely white Revolutionary Communist Party, the American affiliate of Peru's Shining Path guerrillas, did join in on the first night, but it was utterly peripheral to the main action. Those who used the word "uprising" were right in one regard, however. The riot was just a brief, high-intensity episode in a longer-running, low-intensity conflict for which some word with a longer time frame built into it had to be found.

The trouble, increasingly, was that the mass of citizens were on neither side: not, obviously, with the criminals, our urban terrorists, but not quite with the police either. This was the truth that lurked in the welcome given the troops. If an extended occupation could somehow rein in both sides, law-abiding Angelenos of all races would welcome it. (Think how insurance rates would go down!) And most would greatly prefer benign military occupation—or, if you will, a vastly increased community police force—to the wildcat do-it-yourself policing of private gun ownership.

The ratio of police officers to residents in Los Angeles is two to one thousand, the lowest in the nation. And the horizontal immensity of the city's geography further complicates its policing problems. Los Angeles deploys fifteen officers per square mile, as compared with eighty-nine per square mile in New York. Changing the city's numbers would cost money, and neither liberalism nor conservativism has had the will even to make the cast for the change. Liberalism wants to spend tax money on other needs first. Conservatism doesn't want to spend money on anything, not even public safety.

One of the first tasks of an occupying force, if we had one, would be disarmament. I dream of a house-by-house search for illegal arms. But we have no such occupying force, and we aren't likely to get one. On the day of his swearing-in, Police Chief Williams found himself in a public disagreement with Mayor Tom Bradley over whether the city could afford to increase its police force. Days after that, because of a catastrophic revenue shortfall at the state level, the question shifted to whether there would have to be a cut.

The smaller and weaker the police force grows, the greater the domestic arms race among the citizens. Gun shops were among the businesses looted during the riot. Thousands of stolen firearms were added to the hundreds of thousands already in circulation. Legal gun sales, as noted, jumped dramatically after the riot. The National Rifle Association has been running large display ads in newspapers offering free instruction to new gun owners.

Two weeks after the riot David Freed, an investigative reporter, published an extraordinary five-part series in the *Times* on guns in Los Angeles. Eighteen months earlier Freed had published a similar long and chilling series on law enforcement and justice in the city, entitled "Justice in Distress: The Devaluation of Crime in Los Angeles." Its conclusions were that a criminal here stands a small chance of being apprehended, if apprehended a small chance of being convicted, if convicted a small chance of serving a full sentence. In brief, the city appears to be essentially unpoliced. In the new series he was drawing a matching portrait of the public reaction, criminal and otherwise, to that astounding state of affairs. This time, as before, the statistics he marshaled were simply staggering. The rate of death from gunshot homicides in Los Angeles had been less than half the rate of vehicular death in 1970. In 1991 it exceeded that rate. Vehicular safety had improved somewhat, matching the national trend, but the gunshot-homicide rate had tripled: from 464 to 1,554 per 100,000. As for nonfatal shootings, they are so numerous that victims are interviewed briefly or not at all. Strikingly, the understaffed LAPD rarely attempts to trace a weapon. Over the past five years, Freed reported, "466,453 handguns were sold legally in Los Angeles County, one for every nineteen residents. . . . In San Francisco, handgun sales totaled 20,606—a ratio of one for every thirty-five residents." To these handgun numbers must be added legal sales of rifles and shotguns and also illegal sales of guns of all kinds. And the number of guns sold in any way over a five-year period obviously does not equal the total number of guns in circulation.

The influence of guns on ordinary life in Los Angeles is pervasive and profoundly linked to race. During the days following the riot, blacks complained that they were treated with a tense, elaborate politeness when their fellow citizens couldn't avoid them altogether, but avoidance was the preferred strategy. Los Angeles begins at a low level of mutual understanding. The interracial hyperpoliteness whose artificiality offends many blacks is only a heightened form of the city's notorious laid-back manner. The superficiality of Angeleno conversation, so striking to Europeans, is a defensiveness born of experience: blandness as a proactive coloration. One's conversation partner, after all, may be a follower of anyone from Swami Prabhupada to Charles Manson. Why provoke him when for all you know he is not just odd but armed? The diffuse paranoia of a city where so little is shared in the way of common history or securely held values is especially vulnerable to exacerbation by a real-life menace that is both acute and mobile. The automobile, every Angeleno's coat of mail, was no protection from the mob. As all the world knows, motorists were pulled from their vehicles and beaten or killed during the riot.

The entertainment leviathan feeds on this paranoia. Time Warner, the producer of *Body Count,* whose jacket art included a black fist holding a revolver pointed at the viewer, also produced *Lethal Weapon 3.* But conservative politics feeds on the same paranoia. By midsummer George Bush, Dan Quayle, some sixty and mostly Republican congressmen, and the National Rifle Association had all joined the call for a Time Warner boycott. The Time Warner shareholders managed to face down two blinded police officers who addressed their meeting. Though one could feel sorry for them, freedom of artistic expression was a noble tradition, and then, too, profits were up. But when a pension fund decided to divest itself of Time Warner stock, internal dissent grew, and Ice-T, late in July, announced that he had asked his producer to reissue *Body Count* without the offending cut. The result was a spurt in popularity for what is now a collector's item. Meanwhile, Daryl Gates's memoir, *Chief: My Life in the LAPD,* rode high on the *Los Angeles Times* best-seller list for weeks.

A New Paradigm: Black vs. Latinos

For all the compelling power of the Watts II paradigm, however, for all the relevance of white violence and black rage, something still more powerful was happening, and the Latino population of Southern California was at the heart of it.

About a month after the riot a friend sent me a copy of an unsigned editorial from a Mexican-American newspaper, *La Prensa San Diego,* dated May 15. What other Latinos had begun to insinuate, *La Prensa* angrily spelled out: Blacks were not victims. Latinos were victims. Blacks were perpetrators.

> Though confronted with catastrophic destruction of the Latino businesses, which were 60 percent of the businesses destroyed, major looting by blacks and by the Central Americans living in the immediate area and a substantial number of Hispanics being killed, shot and/or injured, every major television station was riveted to the concept that the unfolding events could only be understood if viewed in the context of the black and white experiences. They missed the crucial point: the riots were not carried out against blacks or whites; they were carried out against the Latino and Asian communities by the blacks!
>
> What occurred was a major racial confrontation by the black community, which now sees its numbers and influence waning.

Faced with nearly a million and a half Latinos taking over the inner city, blacks revolted, rioted, and looted. Whatever measure of power and influence they had pried loose from the white power structure, they now see as being in danger of being transferred to the Latino community. Not only are they losing influence, public offices, and control of the major civil rights mechanisms, they now see themselves being replaced in the pecking order by the Asian community, in this case the Koreans.

The editorial ended by declaring "the established Mexican-American communities" to be "the bridge between black, white, Asian, and Latinos." It said, "They will have to bring an end to class, color, and ethnic warfare. To succeed, they will have to do what the blacks failed to do; incorporate all into the human race and exclude no one."

There was, to put it mildly, little in that editorial to suggest that desperately poor, fifteenth-generation African Americans might be within their rights to resent sudden, strong, officially tolerated competition from first-generation Latin Americans and Asian-Americans. But *La Prensa*'s anger clearly arose not just from the riot, perhaps not mainly from the riot, but from frustration at television's inability to see Latin Americans as part of the main action at all.

I don't think that any clear pattern of blacks attacking Latino businesses or Latinos attacking black businesses can be established. Koreans do plainly seem to have been singled out for attack—by some Latinos as well as by many blacks. But state officials believe that at least 30 percent of the approximately four thousand businesses destroyed were Latin-owned. Both "*Somos Hermanos*" and "Black-Owned Business" were frail armor even when those labels were honestly applied. As the police reestablished control, thousands of arrests were made; more than half of the arrestees were Latinos, but the older, second-generation, law-abiding Mexican-American community resented the lack of differentiation in the label "Latino." This community insisted with some feeling that in the communities it regarded as truly and more or less exclusively its own, there had been no rioting. By implication this was the beginning of an anti-immigrant stance within the community.

What counts for more, however, than any incipient struggle between older and newer Latino immigrants is the emerging struggle between Latinos and blacks. *La Prensa* is right to stress the raw size of the Latino population. The terms of engagement, if we take our cue from the rappers, would seem to be black versus white or black versus Asian. But the Korean population of Los Angeles County is just 150,000, a tiny fraction of the Latino population of 3.3 million. Of the 60,560 people in Koreatown itself, only 26.5 percent are Asian; more than 50 percent are Latino. Blacks are the most oppressed minority, but it matters enormously that whites are no longer a majority. And within the urban geography of Los Angeles, African Americans seem to me to be competing more directly with Latin Americans than with any other group.

I find paradoxical confirmation for this view in the fact that some of the most responsible leaders in both groups want to head it off. A month after the riot my wife and I received the June newsletter of the Southern California Interfaith Taskforce on Central America, a group to which we have contributed a little money over the past several years. SCITCA, originally a lobby for the victims of state-sponsored violence in (principally) El Salvador and Guatemala, has more recently expanded its agenda to include the fate of Central Americans now settled in Los Angeles. It has effectively lobbied, for example, for a relaxation of the municipal regulation of street vendors.

In the wake of the riot SCITCA was worried about anti-immigrant backlash. Joe Hicks, of the Southern Christian

Leadership Conference, and Frank Acosta, of the Coalition for Humane Immigrant Rights of Los Angeles, wrote in the newsletter:

> In the aftermath of the recent civil unrest. . . . immigrants and refugees in particular have been targeted for blame, violence, and civil rights abuses. . . . Fears of overcrowding, the burden on local communities, competition for scarce jobs, drainage on public resources through the education and social welfare systems are all commonly held apprehensions about the impact of immigrants in our communities. Similar fears were voiced during the migration of African Americans from the South to the northern cities earlier this century. In the past few years, however, a growing number of social scientists, economists, and researchers have concluded that the social and economic impact of immigration is overwhelmingly positive. By and large, it is the prospect of freedom and economic opportunity, not welfare, that draws immigrants to the state.

Hicks and Acosta were astute to recognize that the movement of millions of blacks from the rural South to the urban North was a migration as enormous as any from abroad, but the fate of those black immigrants and the cities that received them rather subverts the lesson the two writers want to draw. And alongside the recent, pro-immigration literature that the two cite is a small but growing body of even more recent literature suggesting that whether we will it or not, America's older black poor and newer brown poor are on a collision course.

A married couple, both white, both psychiatric social workers in the Los Angeles Unified School District, recently told us of several monolingual school social workers who had been let go to make room for bilingual workers. With so many Spanish speakers in the district, the rationale for requiring social workers to have a knowledge of Spanish is clear. Our friends have, in fact, been diligently studying the language to protect their own positions. And yet it struck them as tragically shortsighted that most of the dismissed social workers were black.

A member of our church administers a subsidized day-care center in northwest Pasadena, once a black neighborhood, now, like South Central Los Angeles, an extremely overcrowded black and Latino neighborhood. Black welfare mothers, our friend reports, are increasingly turned away from the center, because on the neediest-first principle they no longer qualify. Latino mothers, often with more children than the blacks and with no income even from welfare, are needier, and claim a growing share of the available places. Are the Latino mothers illegal? Are they just ill-equipped to apply for welfare? The kindly day-care people don't ask.

Hicks and Acosta exhort: "The poor communities of Los Angeles cannot get caught up fighting over the peanuts that have been given to them by the economic, political, and educational institutions of America." But even if these communities make common political cause, do they have any choice about economic competition? The General Accounting Office reports that janitorial firms serving downtown Los Angeles have almost entirely replaced their unionized black workforce with nonunionized immigrants.

If you live here, you don't need the General Accounting Office to bring you the news. The almost total absence of black gardeners, busboys, chambermaids, nannies, janitors, and construction workers in a city with a notoriously large pool of unemployed, unskilled black people leaps to the eye. According to the U.S. Census, 8.6 percent of South Central Los Angeles residents sixteen years old and older were unemployed in 1990, but an additional 41.8 percent were listed as "not in the labor force." If the Latinos were not around to do that work, nonblack employers would be forced to hire blacks—but they'd rather not. They trust Latinos. They fear or disdain blacks. The result is unofficial but widespread preferential hiring of Latinos—the largest affirmative-action program in the nation, and one paid for, in effect, by blacks.

Pierre Venant, a French photographer of international reputation, made the acquaintance of Father Greg Boyle, a Jesuit who until recently worked in a part of the barrio so badly wracked by gang violence that funerals are held almost weekly. Out of a desire to help Father Boyle, Venant began teaching photography in the barrio and photographing gang members and their sometimes exceedingly elaborate, mural-sized, almost liturgical graffiti. I asked him once whether he had ever considered teaching in the black ghetto. He answered no, that there was something so nihilistic, so utterly alienated, in the black youths he had met that he doubted he could make a connection with them. He was apologetic but plain: it was just easier with the Mexicans. "Maybe it is the Catholicism," he said, "or something in the Latin personality."

The Comfort Factor

I am afraid that quiet choices like Venant's have by now been made so many thousands of times in Los Angeles that, at least to Anglos, Latinos, even when they are foreign, seem native and safe, while blacks, who are native, seem foreign and dangerous. In saying this, I am saying something that I shrink from saying and grieve to say, but I think it's true. As a graduate student at Harvard, I shared an apartment with a Nigerian, and I learned to measure by the ease and speed of my rapport with him, despite immense cultural differences (he had been raised in a polygamous family), how deep an estrangement separated me from African Americans. For a time I helped to administer Harvard's Big Brothers program, which teamed freshmen, almost always white, with fatherless boys, almost always black, from the Columbia Point Housing Project. I spent a lot of time during that period with black people, and this in the 1960s, when interracial hope and goodwill were at flood tide. But in the end I felt that even with me they were prepared at every moment, at every single moment, for the worst—braced, as it were, for a blow. This is what slavery has done to us as a people, and I can scarcely think of it without tears.

Every other week since the riot a team made up of parishioners from my church, St. Edmund's, in San Marino, and from St. Martin's, in Compton, has distributed food to needy people in Compton. One of the albums of the rap group N.W.A. (the name stands for "Niggers With Attitude") is entitled "Straight Outta Compton." Compton, a town in the South Central area of greater Los Angeles, has replaced Watts, a Los Angeles neighborhood, as a byword for black anger, and not just because of that album. But the people we see meekly filing past for their shopping bags of free food are more often old than young and, to my eyes, more weary than angry. Black writers since at least Richard Wright's day have noted with bitterness how white America smiles on cute black children and the benign black elderly, while the prime-of-life adults of the black community and, above all, its young males are objects of white dread. Times have changed, at least some: Arsenio Hall, Eddie Murphy— if not niggers with attitude, then undeniably African Americans with panache—would have been inconceivable in Wright's day. And yet I still caught myself being surprised— and then chagrined at my surprise—to see how frail some of our "customers" were. I was particularly struck by an old, bent black man wearing a bright green DAY LABORERS' UNION windbreaker. He wasn't up for much in the way of day labor, but when he had been young and strong, had he been a union man? What had happened to his union? And to his hopes? These are the black people nobody but other black people ever really sees and nobody but other black people ever stops to think about.

And yet . . .

My wife and I sold the trailer in 1986 and bought a small

house in an unincorporated chunk of Los Angeles County, adjacent to Pasadena on the east. Of twenty households on our block, one is Asian (Chinese), two African American, and one Latino (he is Puerto Rican, she is Mexican). None of the houses on the block is large enough to accommodate live-in help, but several of us do employ gardeners. All the gardeners are Latino, and when a slight brown man walks down a driveway, he is understood to be there for good reason. Were a tall black man to do the same, there is not one of us who would not immediately be on the *qui vive*. My sadness about the American estrangement just mentioned doesn't make me act any differently at such a moment.

Black men complain that they cannot shop without being shadowed by a suspicious shopkeeper. The same in effect goes for the black teenagers who show up unannounced on our block. These are kids who skip out of the junior high school in the next block, picnic on our lawns, steal from our garages and backyards, and occasionally vandalize parked cars. The retirees living on the block watch the kids especially closely. One retiree once managed to videotape an attempted garage break-in. The school's officials—not always sympathetic (until recently the principal was a black woman)—identified the culprits from the tape.

We, who live peacefully with the black families on our block, are afraid of these black kids. I contrast our attitude toward them with the attitude taken in neighboring Sierra Madre, almost completely white and Republican, toward a group of as many as twenty Latino men who gather each morning except Sunday in a park near the fire department. They are day laborers, the poorest of the poor, awaiting work. In principle (and especially toward the demoralizing end of a day when no one has hired them), they ought to be desperate, but they are in the main clean, quiet, mannerly, polite to the residents, and agreeably fraternal with one another. This very conservative, old-fashioned community tolerates their presence calmly.

Whether or not Latinos are completely trustworthy (I

have already mentioned the bloody barrio gang wars), I think that they do enjoy the trust of Anglos and Asians in Los Angeles. In the yard, in the house, with the baby, in the hotel room or the hotel corridor, in the parking garage, in a hundred locations, work, however menial, creates a vulnerability and thereby a brief intimacy between server and served. In all these places the average white or Asian Angeleno prefers to have—and usually does have—a Latino rather than an African American doing the work. Whence at least some of the disorientation and diffuse anxiety at the television footage of rioting Latinos: Had that young man dashing out of the liquor store been in your backyard earlier in the week? Was that woman trundling a shopping cart of looted groceries out of the supermarket your neighbor's live-out? ("Live-out" is Angeleno for a domestic servant who works for you five or six days a week, all day, but doesn't sleep over.)

I do not discount, as I mention this "comfort factor," that inexperienced Latino noncitizens may be much easier to exploit than experienced black citizens. Ricky was hired at less than the minimum wage to do drywall plastering on Santa Monica condominiums that sold for more than $1 million each. The contractor trained him on the job. Ricky learns quickly, and his by then confident bilingualism was a major plus for his employer. He was promised a "real" job after this unofficial apprenticeship ended, but no such job ever materialized. His brother Victor, who owns a car, worked briefly for a messenger service. He was required to use his own car. No mileage, insurance, or fuel costs were paid by his employer. He was paid by the mile only when actually delivering a package, but was required to keep himself available for an assignment even when none was forthcoming. The Latinos I know think that Asians are particularly likely to cheat and brutalize their Latino employees in ways like these.

And I do not mean, either, to sanctify Latinos at the expense of blacks. Victor called me as I was writing this article to report that Miguel, "Mike," the youngest brother in the family, was about to get out of jail. Ricky is also in jail as I write, and one of his earlier criminal ventures began with my wife. Near the end of Ricky's senior year his mother told me that he was dejected because he couldn't afford to attend the prom: no car and no money to rent a tux. I said I would rent the tux for him. My wife, who had just bought a used Honda and hadn't yet sold her 1969 Volkswagen, agreed to lend him the VW for the occasion. He had a good time at the prom but didn't return the car for two days. Graduation came a few weeks later. (The commencement speaker was State Senator Art Torres, whose remarks were all about Latino progress, but when the awards were given out, the few Asians in the student body won them all.) By custom, on the day after graduation local high school seniors head for Magic Mountain, an amusement park. Ricky asked to borrow the car again. We were already planning to sell it to him and let him pay us in installments from his first job. He was prematurely developing a proprietary attitude toward it. My wife had a premonition. I overrode it. He stole the car and skipped town.

The odd consequence of this episode was an intensification of my relationship with Ricky's family, especially his mother. The police, once they knew the car had been "borrowed for keeps," wouldn't list it as stolen. But if I couldn't call it stolen, I couldn't get it off my insurance policy. I had to gamble that if Ricky's ties to us were breakable, his ties to his family were not. It worked. Ricky eventually returned the car, and afterward even paid us $250 for it—less than it was worth but, given his resources, a meaningful gesture.

By that time we had a new baby in the house, and we lost touch with the Rodríguez family—until a few years later, when Victor called to invite us to his wedding. Ricky, who had been working as a house painter near Sacramento, was back in Los Angeles, nattily dressed and doing well, it seemed, as a salesman in a car dealership. Victor spoke of him with a kind of relief. But some months after the wedding Ricky and Victor's sister Elena called to ask, on behalf of their mother, if I would stand bail. Ricky had been stopped on a traffic charge, and a computer check showed that he was wanted for parole violation in the north. I declined, but later, on an trip to Sacramento, I visited him in the minimum-security jail where he was serving his sentence. I learned then that during his first northern period he had become a father. The child, a boy, was being raised by its mother and her parents, Anglos with whom Ricky claimed to be on friendly terms, though clearly all contact had been lost. After his release from jail Ricky moved in with Victor, Victor's wife, and their new baby, but within weeks he had been arrested again, this time on a drug charge. When Victor called about Mike, he said that Ricky, too, would be out in a month or two.

Sometimes, as I have reflected on our checkered ten-year friendship with the Rodríguez family, I have wondered whether Latinos do not have a better local reputation, and blacks a worse one, than each deserves. But how much difference does reputation ultimately make? True, walking the streets of downtown Los Angeles, I do not expect to be panhandled or shaken down (the two grow increasingly similar) by Latinos; I do fear that from blacks. True, I am wary of black men and generally nonchalant with Latinos. I think my attitudes are typical. And yet, all that aside, if there were no Latinos—and no other immigrants—around to do all the work that is to be done in Los Angeles, would blacks not be hired to do it? I think they would be. Wages might have to be raised. Friction might be acute for a while. But in the end the work would go looking for available workers.

Labor's View: The Rodney King Riot as a Bread Riot

I am not alone in thinking so. In July 1992 the Black Leadership Forum, a coalition headed by Coretta Scott King and Walter E. Fauntroy and including Jack Otero, the president of the Labor Council for Latin American Advancement, wrote to Senator Orrin Hatch urging him not to repeal the sanctions imposed on employers of illegal aliens under the Immigration Reform and Control Act of 1986. "We are concerned, Senator Hatch," the group wrote,

> that your proposed remedy to the employer sanctions–based discrimination, namely, the elimination of employer sanctions, will cause another problem—the revival of the pre-1986 discrimination against black and brown U.S. and documented workers, in favor of cheap labor—the undocumented workers. This would undoubtedly exacerbate an already severe economic crisis in communities where there are large numbers of new immigrants.

Labor leaders like Otero and another cosigner, William Lucy, of the Coalition of Black Trade Unionists, are notoriously critical of free trade, especially to the negotiation of a free-trade agreement between the United States and Mexico. Their opposition to lax enforcement of immigration law, which creates a free trade in labor, is only consistent. What difference is there between exporting jobs and importing workers?

The politics of labor and immigration makes strange bedfellows. On most issues the Southern California Interfaith Taskforce on Central America is an extremely liberal group, but on employer sanctions it sides with Senator Hatch. In effect, SCITCA would rather see wages go down and its Central American clients have work of some kind than see wages stay high and penniless refugees be left with nothing. La Placita, the Mission Church of Our Lady Queen of Angels, near downtown Los Angeles, became for a time a sanctuary for illegal hiring.

Latino immigrants at the bottom of the labor market often claim to be doing work that "Americans" refuse to do. Are they thinking of black Americans? It may not matter.

Commenting to a *New York Times* reporter on the extremely low employment rate for sixteen- to nineteen-year-olds in New York City in early 1992—12.6 percent—Vernon M. Briggs, a labor economist at Cornell University, said, "To an immigrant willing to work two or three jobs at once, five dollars an hour may not look bad. But to a kid from Brooklyn or the Bronx, it is a turnoff." To some of their parents these kids seem to be prima donnas, but in fact the influx of immigrants willing to work long hours for low wages has depressed wages and increased competition beyond anything that the parents ever faced. And the attitudinal difference between unskilled Americans of any race and their immigrant competition shrinks as the immigrants gain a clearer view of what faces them in the United States.

During his buoyant junior year at Wilson High School, Ricky carried a pocket dictionary. One day he told me that he had come upon an entry that had shaken him to his roots: *happy-go-lucky*. "That's my problem," he said. "I'm happy-go-lucky." Ricky's merry, open-faced manner was one of his greatest assets, but I think I know what he meant. I had often marveled that a boy up against so much could remain so high-spirited. I now think that he simply hadn't yet realized how much he was up against. Tension grew between him and Victor after his first release from jail. Victor wanted Ricky to take a job, any job, just to be working: dishwasher, gardener's helper, anything. Ricky drew the line at that kind of work. He was able to do rough carpentry, drywall work, simple plumbing. Besides his building skills, he was completely bilingual and could even write surprisingly coherent and error-free English. "I am an educated man," he said to me in a choked voice. Both words counted. Ricky was arrested again on a drug charge, but he has never been addicted. He was dealing, and he was dealing because as he had grown more American, he had grown impatient. "Ricky wanted money. That's what got him into trouble," Victor says. Jorge G. Castañeda put it differently in an op-ed piece in the *Times*:

In Mexico and El Salvador, with the exception of the role played by the church in the latter country a few years ago, poverty and inequality did not outrage its victims, nor did it lead them to violence. . . . But the same deprivation, with the same inequities, in a radically different context, produces different effects. Poverty and injustice were not supposed to be the same: the United States was the land of social mobility, well-paid work, and unlimited opportunities. Not any more. A Latin American migrant's future is often the same as his current reality: $4.50 an hour for unskilled labor for the rest of his or her life, maybe with a raise to $6 or $7 an hour, eventually.

But the young Mexicans or Salvadorans who do housework in Beverly Hills, garden in Bel-Air or park Jags and BMWs for restaurants on Melrose had no idea this is what awaited them when they left Usulután or Guanajuato. And the ideological bombardment they are now subjected to no longer helps them accept matters as they are. On the contrary, it incites rejection, indignation, and class hatred. Any spark can light the fire.

So, yes. Latinos compete with blacks for work at the bottom, but they also match them in rejecting $4.50 an hour as chump change. And then what? Then, among other things, readiness for a bread riot (a cake riot, if you will) in which the disappointed, by the thousands, steal what they once thought they could earn.

The question of how immigrant groups may fit into the American economy without dislodging or otherwise adversely affecting native groups is itself contained in the larger question of how an American economy carrying all these groups within it can compete against other national economies. In an article given wide distribution by the Federation for American Immigration Reform (FAIR), Vernon Briggs claims that immigration accounts for 30 to 35 percent of the annual growth of the American labor force, a proportion virtually unknown elsewhere in the industrialized world. In 1989, Briggs writes, "the total number of immigrants from all sources admitted for permanent residence was 1,090,924—the highest figure for any single year since 1914 (and this figure did not include any estimate of the additional illegal immigrant flow or of the number of nonimmigrants permitted to work in the United States on a temporary basis during that year)."

The immigration story becomes the riot story by becoming a part of the labor story. And by an irony that I find particularly cruel, unskilled Latino immigration may be doing to American blacks at the end of the twentieth century what the European immigration that brought my own ancestors here did to them at the end of the nineteenth. Briggs writes,

> When the industrialization process began in earnest during the later decades of the nineteenth century, the newly introduced technology of mechanization required mainly unskilled workers to fill manufacturing jobs in the nation's expanding urban labor markets. The same can be said of the other employment growth sectors of mining, construction, and transportation. Pools of citizen workers existed who could have been incorporated to meet those needs—most notably the recently freed blacks of the former slave economies of the rural South. But mass immigration from Asia and Europe became the chosen alternative.

The chosen alternative: those are the words that should disturb our sleep. People do not blow into our country like the weather. We let them in, and we have reasons for doing so. Or we should. In my city, on my own block, in my own house, I have seen the immigrant Latino alternative being chosen over the native black one.

But this is only the beginning of the problem. I am talking about a mistake that is now, as it were, complete. Blacks in Los Angeles have been largely closed out of the unskilled-labor market; the earlier-arriving Latinos are now competing with the later-arriving Latinos. This is the embarrassing fact that *La Prensa* seemed so little able to face and that has led lately to a Latino Unity Forum. Briggs makes disturbing reading on the consequences of increasing the pool of unskilled applicants while the pool of jobs shrinks:

> No technologically advanced industrial nation that has 27 million illiterate and another 20–40 million marginally literate adults need fear a shortage of unskilled workers in its foreseeable future. Indeed, immigration—especially that of illegal immigrants, recent amnesty recipients, and refugees—is a major contributor to the growth of adult illiteracy in the United States. To this degree, immigration, by adding to the surplus of illiterate adult job seekers, is serving to diminish the limited opportunities for poorly prepared citizens to find jobs or to improve their employability by on-the-job training. It is not surprising, therefore, that the underground economy is thriving in many urban centers. Moreover the nature of the overall immigration and refugee flow is also contributing to the need for localities to expand funding for remedial education and training and language programs in many urban communities. Too often these funding choices cause scarce public funds to be diverted from being used to upgrade the human resource capabilities of the citizen labor force.

Briggs's analysis seems to me to make a mockery of the brave talk of a Los Angeles "recovery." What does it mean for the city to recover in an American society that is adding at least 700,000 immigrants a year to its population? The official "Rebuild L.A." coalition, headed by Peter Ueberroth, the former director of the 1984 Los Angeles Olympics and the former commissioner of baseball, will be hard-enough pressed to cope just with the city's share of those new workers. Assimilating so many new workers while reassimilating the thousands left jobless by the riot may well be more than the economy could handle even in a boom period, and southern California is still deep in recession. The recession may mean that fewer Americans will move to the state, but if San Diego County statistics for 1990–91 are any indication, foreign immigration may not be similarly slowed. In that period net domestic in-migration was just 427, a steep plunge in comparison with the increases of earlier years, but foreign immigration held steady at 19,442.

And competition for goods other than employment is more acute during a recession than at any other time. The Center for Immigration Studies estimates that direct public-assistance and education costs at all levels of government for immigrants and refugees entering the United States in calendar year 1990 totaled $2.2 billion. Immigrants and refugees made up 1.3 percent of the caseload of Medi-Cal, California's state-paid health care, in 1980; the California Department of Finance estimates that they will make up 13 percent by the turn of the century. The administrative office of the Los Angeles County Board of Supervisors reported in the spring of last year that federal costs for the citizen children of ineligible alien parents, including Medicaid and Aid to Families with Dependent Children, had risen from approximately $57.7 million in 1988–89 to $140.5 million in 1990–91 and could reach $533 million by the year 2000. If the burden of that welfare grows too great, another tax revolt could take place, and another safety valve could be removed from places like South Central Los Angeles.

Few Californians are aware, I think, of how many public school seats are filled by illegal immigrants. But as awareness grows, the already eroded support for public education at all levels may erode further. Nonimmigrant whites are still the majority in the state, and older whites—whose children may be grown—still turn out to vote more reliably than any other group. True, only some of the Asians burning up the track at the University of California are immigrants, but more are the children of immigrants. When whites in Berkeley's freshman class dropped to 30 percent, there was talk of a cooling of white support for the costly nine-campus system. As for the larger, more teaching-oriented California State University, it has never charged noncitizens legally resident in California a higher tuition; but a recent decision by Alameda County Superior Court Judge Ken Kawaichi now requires that illegal aliens receive the same generous treatment.

By July 1, 1993, when a budget impasse for fiscal 1992–93 forced California to begin paying many of its bills with scrip instead of money, some of the bitterest infighting had touched the third and nationally least known of the state's higher-education systems, the gigantic California Community Colleges system, with its 1.5 million enrollment. Would the heaviest community college cuts come in short-term vocational education, hurting blacks disproportionately? Or would continuing education take the hit, hurting older white women returning to the work force? Little noticed in public comment on the budget battle was the fact that immigrants constituted 10 percent of 1990–91 community college enrollment. California was providing all-but-free higher education, in other words, to 150,000 immigrant undergraduates. For comparison, Harvard and Radcliffe together enroll fewer than 7,000 undergraduates. The community college system has to be regarded as a de facto incentive for immigration—a GI Bill for people who were never GIs, as I once heard it described. If and when free higher education for immigrants, especially illegal immigrants, comes under attack, however, free elementary and high school education for them will most inevitably come into question as well. And the social dislocation lurking in the latter question is almost incalculable.

In March 1992 *Science* published a research report by

Georges Vernez and David Ronfeldt on Mexican immigration. The evidence in the report shows that recent immigrants are those who feel the greatest economic impact from still more recent immigrants. And because Mexican immigrants tend to be young and to have large families, they consume more in public services, especially educational ones, than they pay for. The researchers say that both the absolute size of the Mexican-immigrant population and its relative concentration in Los Angeles and several other western cities are growing.

Vernez and Ronfeldt also argue that "heavy immigration into California . . . let many low-wage industries continue expanding while their counterparts nationwide were contracting in the face of foreign competition." Their data show that in California manufacturing grew five times the national average whereas wages grew 12 percent more slowly in the state, and 15 percent more slowly in Los Angeles. The implications for labor are clear: either manufacturing is exported to take advantage of cheap foreign labor, or cheap foreign labor is imported in numbers large enough to depress wages here. Open borders create a free trade in labor, and America's southern border, though not open by law, has been open enough in practice to move the Los Angeles labor market sharply away from the American mean.

Do we like it this way?

The short answer might be yes if we want more riots, no if we don't.

In his book *Los Angeles: Capital of the Third World,* David Rieff charges that white Los Angeles has grown addicted to the ministrations of a Latino "servitor class," and there is something in his charge. In 1985 my wife and I paid sixty-five dollars a week to a licensed, well-educated, decidedly middle-class Peruvian couple who cared beautifully for several infants and toddlers in a home they owned. Our newborn daughter was typically with them from 7:30 A.M. to 6:00 P.M. five days a week. My younger sister, who lives in

Skokie, a suburb of Chicago, found this at the time an incredible bargain, and so it has seemed to New Yorkers and Washingtonians as well. Thus I no doubt fit Rieff's definition of white Angeleno indulgence myself.

The larger beneficiaries of cheap labor, however, seem to me to be the larger employers. Ricky's sisters Dolores and Graciela worked in a sweatshop assembling those little gadgets—two plastic eyelets joined by a length of cord—that tennis players use to keep their eyeglasses on. There were huge spools of the cord and barrels of the eyelets in the private home (of an Italian married to a Costa Rican) where they worked. And the profits from that little operation were surely peanuts compared with those made on the luxury condos where Ricky did his drywall work.

Obviously, Los Angeles should want to maintain a manufacturing base, large and small. But if the price is systematically depressed wages, and if the price of that depression is further riots, then the price is too high.

Will Immigration Be Reformed?

Just days before the riot, the Roper Organization conducted a major poll of American attitudes toward immigration for FAIR, the Federation for American Immigration Reform. On every single question for which the California response was broken out, the level of concern in California was higher—often strikingly higher—than the American average. Thus 76 percent of Californians answering the question "How do you feel about the number of immigrants who come to your state each year?" answered "Too high," as against 42 percent of all respondents giving the same answer. Answering the question "In your opinion, has immigration become a financial burden on your state, or has the state been able to handle the immigration with no financial problems?," 78 percent of Californians, as against 43 percent of all respondents, chose "financial burden." Eighty percent of Californians think that steps should be taken now to limit the population of the state (a question that Roper put only to Californians).

FAIR has an agenda, of course, and polls by people with an agenda are always suspect. However, the Roper Organization is reputable, and the questions are more or less those that anyone interested in the subject would ask, phrased in acceptably neutral language. Thus, "Currently, immigration levels are not limited in any way to our country's unemployment rate. Do you think immigration levels *should* or *should not* be related to our level of unemployment?" Fifty-eight percent of respondents chose "Should be related." (Roper did not indicate whether any respondents corrected "limited" to "linked.")

FAIR is anathema to some, but better a clearly framed agenda, however debatable, than free-range nativism.

Some days after the riot I caught a fragment of televised debate between a handsome blond man of unsmiling, quasi-military demeanor, a proponent of a return to the pro-European quotas of the Immigration Act of 1924, and a Mexican-American activist of the Aztlán persuasion. Responding to the claim that the Southwest "was once ours," the young Aryan said, "Yes, and we took it from you in the manly, honorable way, by force of arms." A writer in the July 1992 issue of the Rockford Institute's *Chronicles: A Magazine of American Culture* laments the intrusion of immigrants who "have no more intention of shucking the Third World they've lugged across the border than they have of going back after they make their millions. Once here, they're here for good, disrupting our institutions, like public schools, with foreign languages, pagan religions, and oddly spiced foods."

FAIR holds no brief for manliness, Christianity, or bland food. Nor, for that matter, does it oppose immigration. What it does call for is a three-year moratorium, or however long it takes to:

1. substantially eliminate illegal immigration;
2. implement and improve a national documents protocol to verify work eligibility;
3. revise immigration laws to substantially reduce overall numbers (to around 300,000 annually); and
4. complete a comprehensive analysis of the long-term demographic, environmental resource, urban resource, cultural, and employment/economic effects of future immigration and population growth.

Ultimately, this question must be answered: what should the purpose of immigration be, now and in the future?

I link FAIR's question with the phrase of Vernon Briggs's that so struck me: "the chosen alternative." There are choices to be made. If we do not make them as a nation, through a national debate, then others inside or outside the nation will make them for us. My strong suspicion is that if FAIR succeeds in launching this debate, it will begin on the right (immigration was the cover story in the June 22, 1993, issue of *National Review*) but quickly be seized by the left. The labels "left" and "right," however, are particularly misleading here.

If the right opposes immigration, it is likely to do so for the reasons hinted at in the quotation from *Chronicles* and on display as well in the *National Review* article, by Peter Brimelow: namely, because it wishes the United States to remain a culturally European and even English nation. The free-market right wing, however—the right that has favored a free-trade agreement with Mexico—ought to favor open borders as the logical extension of the open shop. This is indeed the declared position of the *Wall Street Journal*. Such a position may be more ideologically consistent than politically feasible, but it is not without its supporters. Too many business interests have been served by cheap immigrant labor for any Buchananesque, shoot-to-kill sealing of our southern border to gain much Republican support. In short, between cultural conservatism and economic conservatism there is a certain tension on this question; but, as noted above, the situation is equally messy for liberals. If you marched with Amnesty International in Los Angeles on June 27, 1993, denouncing the border excesses of the Immigration and Naturalization Service, then do you positively—proactively, as they say—favor immigration? FAIR would admit 300,000 immigrants a year. How many would you admit? And if blacks get hurt, whose side are you on?

The traditional alliances grow particularly shaky in a climate of budget crisis like the current one in California. As I write, if California public education receives what Governor Pete Wilson budgeted for it in January 1993, and if current revenue projections remain unchanged, then all other government services will have to shrink drastically. Mayor Bradley has warned of a total shutdown of the Los Angeles Public Library. Few believe that will happen, but if all ordinary deals are off, then some unlikely deals may be on.

FAIR has proposed, for example, a two-dollar border-crossing fee to finance strengthened border security. According to the Roper poll, 72 percent of Californians favor that measure, and I am not surprised. Against them stand those who favor lax border security and some who go further and call for a borderless, European Community–like arrangement. The fee proposal could at least bring the issue to a head. Senator John Seymour has proposed a bill by which the federal government would be fiscally responsible for some or all of the legal costs incurred by illegal aliens, including public defense and incarceration. I'm not so sure that liberals wouldn't back that idea if they thought it would free up some California money for the beleaguered university. Representative Elton Gallegly, a Republican from Simi Valley, has proposed that American citizenship be denied to the U.S.-born children of illegal immigrants. I doubt that many Americans, liberal or conservative, have stopped to consider that not every country establishes citizenship as we do—that is, by place of birth rather than by descent. Perhaps the biggest bombshell would be the imposition of a citizenship requirement for elementary and high school education. I am not aware that anyone has proposed this. But the Los Angeles Unified School District, faced with a $400 million cutback in its state funding for the coming fiscal year, notified its teachers in late July that their pay would be cut by 14 percent, and despite the severity of the economies, the district could conceivably go into receivership—as the Richmond District, near San Francisco, did last year. When such a thing happens, Sacramento is stuck both with a cash bailout and with the task of direct administration—all but impossible in the case of a system with 600,000 students. In such an unthinkable crisis unthinkable remedies might suddenly be thought of.

On June 23, 1993, Tim W. Ferguson published a column on immigration in the *Wall Street Journal,* under the title "The Sleeper Issue of the 1990s Awakens." He is right to summarize the issue thus, and in this sense, at least, I would agree with those who have called the Rodney King riot "a wake-up call." But what may quite possibly happen if the country hears this call is the revival of another sleeper issue—namely, labor. If you want to keep up with labor news in Los Angeles, the way to do it is to read *La Opinion,* the city's major Spanish-language newspaper. The GAO report I mentioned earlier says that during the 1980s the downtown force of hotel workers went from being almost 100 percent black, and organized, to 100 percent immigrant, and nonunion. That report has been overtaken by events during the past five years. The unions are finding that the same Americanization, the same "Where's mine?" impatience, that turned Latinos into rioters can also turn them into strikers. A remarkable shot across the civic bow came when Local 11 of the Hotel and Restaurant Employees Union produced and distributed to convention planners an "attack video" linking a grim portrayal of the dangers of life in Los Angeles to declining wages and deteriorating living conditions for the poor. As Frank Clifford, a *Los Angeles Times* writer, put it: "The message of the video is that the city won't be a nice place for tourists until the tourism business is nicer to its workers." A much improved contract followed with rare speed.

The End of the American Dilemma

Whether or not the immigration debate becomes a labor debate, America may not have the luxury of treating it as merely national issue. Race relations were once the quintessentially domestic American problem—"an American dilemma," as Gunnar Myrdal called it. Immigration, too, a fact everywhere, was a boast here. What other nation had a major monument inscribed "Give me your tired, your poor . . ."? But these points of view have now changed. Because the world has shrunk, migrants don't have to cut all ties to home and cast their cultural and economic lot with us as they once did. If it is possible for an American businessman to have a vacation home in France, it may be possible for a Korean businessman to have a "work home" or a "school home" in America. And if resolving the American dilemma—in other words, instituting a "blacks first" policy—creates a problem for such immigrants, the result may be an international incident, if not a long-running diplomatic problem.

South Korea's government sent a delegation to Los Angeles to request reparations for the burned-out merchants of Koreatown. The presidential candidate Kim Dae Jung came, too, and though he spoke of compensation rather than reparation, his visit, like that of the government delegation, served notice that South Korea needs these merchants and still regards them as its own. Mexico made no comparable gesture, but it is worth noting that of Mexicans who entered the United States during the 1960s, only 21 percent had become citizens by 1980. This kind of statistic is usually cited to explain why Latinos have so little clout in American politics. But the same statistic, given an increase in cross-border tension, could explain why some future Carlos Salinas de Gortari or Cuauhtémoc Cárdenas could become a factor in U.S. domestic affairs as the powerful extraterritorial leader of millions of noncitizen residents of the United States. Any attempt in the interests of American blacks to seal the U.S.-Mexican border and seal in all of Mexico's unemployed would deprive Mexico of a desperately needed safety valve and could foster the rise in that country of a terrorist movement like Peru's Shining Path. In short, America is no longer quite free to address the needs of its own underclass in isolation from similar needs elsewhere in the world.

The spring of 1992 saw both the riot in Los Angeles and the debacle (for the United States) of the United Nations Conference on Environment and Development—the Earth Summit—in Rio de Janeiro. U.S. coverage focused on the environmental half of "Environment and Development." The delegates, however, were at least equally interested in the developmental half, and therefore in the enormous disparity of wealth between the First World and the Third World. It was the reluctance of a Republican administration to submit to a sociopolitical agenda dictated from afar that caused all the difficulty. President Bush sent William K. Reilly, of the Environmental Protection Agency. By rights, he could have sent both Reilly and Jack Kemp, of Housing and Urban Development.

FAIR has an ally of sorts in the United Nations Development Program, where much of the developmental half of the Rio agenda was hatched. Aldo Ajello, the assistant administrator of the program, who visited Los Angeles a month after the riot, is, in his own highly nuanced way, an opponent of immigration. The immigration of selected, well-prepared people can be good both for them and for the country that receives them, he says, but mass immigration of unskilled, unprepared people simply adds the problem of culture shock and maladjustment to the problems the immigrants are fleeing. From the standpoint of a developed country, opening markets to products from a neighboring underdeveloped country that otherwise might be reduced to exporting desperate, surplus people makes good economic sense. So does investing in such a country—for the same reason. Given a choice between exporting jobs and importing people, Ajello urges exporting jobs as the less disruptive alternative.

Because that alternative is not being chosen, he says, and because the General Agreement on Tariffs and Trade actually governs (and frees) only a small fraction of world trade, enormous pressure is building for mass migration—the largest, he thinks, that the world has seen since antiquity. When I pointed out to him that the U.S.-Mexican border is the only land border between a First and Third World country, he countered that Italy has a long, undefended coastline, that crossing from Morocco to Spain (or from Tunisia to Sicily) by boat may be easier than crossing from Haiti to Florida by boat, and that the land border between Western Europe and the former Soviet bloc is in some ways comparable to the U.S.-Mexican border. In the long run, he believes, global development will require open borders as well as truly free trade. As for the short run, "Your choice is the Marshall Plan or martial law." Absent the most severe countermeasures, the increasing disparity of wealth will tend to move people across borders as irresistibly as a low-pressure–high-pressure system moves clouds. The top 20 percent of the world population had thirty times the wealth of the bottom 20 percent in 1960. Today it has 150 times the wealth of the bottom 20 percent. Equalization can come about in only two ways: by immigration or by development; by moving people from the Third World to the First, or by moving capital from the First World to the Third. An American moratorium on immigration might be a defensible temporary expedient, but only if it was accompanied by a compensating increase in investment.

American discussions of immigration tend to focus on pull rather than on push—that is, on those aspects of American life that pull immigrants in rather than on those aspects of life in their native countries that push them out. FAIR might put in place quite an assortment of American disincentives—changes in the pull—without addressing the Third World distress that creates the push. At that point, having declined the Marshall Plan alternative, we might be forced into the martial-law one, and into a particularly severe form of it along our southern border. President Bush was less than eager to visit Los Angeles, and he was particularly loath to dignify the Rio conference with a personal appearance. In the end he could avoid neither, and he was, in effect, visiting two ends of the same globally disruptive process.

The Judgments of the Lord

The same colleague who remembered the sack of Rome as we left the *Times* building, its windows still boarded up, the streets not yet patrolled by the National Guard, had earlier lent me his videotaped copy of the PBS Civil War series. Midway through the writing of this article I concluded my viewing of the series and heard an actor reading Abraham Lincoln's Second Inaugural Address. There is a strange, deep similarity between the logic of angry blacks who called the Rodney King riot understandable and inevitable—and, indeed, barely stopped short of calling it justifiable—and the logic of the man who wrote,

> Fondly do we hope, fervently do we pray, that this mighty scourge of war may speedily pass away. Yet, if God wills that it continue until all the wealth piled up by the bondsman's two hundred and fifty years of unrequited toil shall be sunk, and until every drop of blood drawn with the lash shall be paid by another drawn with the sword, as was said three thousand years ago, so still it might be said, "The judgments of the Lord are true and righteous altogether."

My deepest, least argued or arguable hunch is that every-thing in America begins with that old and still unpaid debt. An America in which it was finally paid, in which blacks were no longer afraid and no one was any longer afraid of blacks—what could such a country not attempt? But if, to quote an ex-slave, all God's dangers ain't the white man, all God's dangers ain't the black man either. The earth, as the century ends, has many wretched, and we are living in their house.

Closed Doors
Richard Rodriguez

Richard Rodriguez is a contributing editor to *Harper's* magazine and an associate editor at Pacific News Service. He is the author of *Hunger of Memory: The Education of Richard Rodriguez* and *Days of Obligation: An Argument with My Mexican Father*. "Closed Doors" first appeared in the *Los Angeles Times*, August 15, 1991.

CALIFORNIANS ARE AFRAID of the future and cannot imagine themselves in the great world. To prove it, Governor Pete Wilson recently published an open letter to President Bill Clinton, urging a constitutional amendment to deny citizenship to the children of illegal immigrants as well as the repeal of federal mandates requiring health and education services for illegal immigrants.

On the same day that the governor published his letter ("on behalf of the people of California"), I was at a chic Los Angeles hotel. All day, I saw Mexicans working, busily working to maintain California's legendary "quality of life." The common complaint of Californians is that the immigrants, whether legally or illegally here, are destroying our quality of life. But there the Mexicans were—hosing down the tiles by the hotel swimming pool, gardening, everywhere gardening. The woman who could barely speak English was making beds; at the Yuppie restaurant, Mexican men impersonated Italian chefs.

Who could accuse Wilson of xenophobia? The governor

was, after all, only concerned with those immigrants illegally here. His presumption was that the illegal immigrants are here only for the umbrella of welfare services. Remove those benefits and they will go back to Mexico, the governor reasoned. Here was a presumption in Wilson's letter that betrayed naïveté about the desperation of the Third World poor and their wild ambition for work.

"God, do they work," a friend confides over martinis in Bel-Air. "I've never seen people work like those Mexicans."

What troubles us about the Mexican immigrant is that she works too hard. The myth California has advertised to the world is that here is a place of leisure—the myth of blond beaches and palm trees. The myth continues: "California was created by "internal immigrants," by Americans from Iowa or Oklahoma or Brooklyn, New York. They came to California in search of a softer winter, an easier America.

In truth, life in Los Angeles today is no more difficult than life in Chicago or Atlanta or New York—but that is not the point. Californians expect life in L.A. to be *easier* than life back East. Native-born Californians remember being able to park in Westwood; they are appalled by the loss of the green hills and by having to wait in line—lines at the grocery store, lines at the DMV, lines on the Santa Monica freeway. California, people say, used to be easier.

It is inevitable that the governor of California would misunderstand, would assume that the Mexicans are coming for welfare. In a state whose most famous industry is entertainment, the desperate Mexican must puzzle us. Desperate immigrants challenge the sunniest myth we have about ourselves and this place. Mexicans, looking for work, would turn Los Angeles into a city like Cleveland or Hong Kong, a Mexican city.

It is embarrassing to watch the Mexican work, like watching a peasant ant. The Mexican, perhaps most especially the illegal immigrant, reminds us how hard life is; he reminds us that in much of this world, one must work or die.

Work becomes life. The feel of work, the assurance of a handle to hold, a hope. The peach is torn from the branch, the knife slits open the fish; the stake is plunged into the earth (faster . . . faster). Work or die. The Mexican works.

Not only are Mexicans working, of course. There are also Vietnamese, Koreans, Guatemalans, Salvadorans, Chinese. Wilson's letter to the President was only concerned with Mexicans and with Mexico, but many Californians probably are made more uneasy with the Asian migration. If, as the governor believes, Mexicans are a burden because they are poor, Asians are a threat because they are poised to take over the city. In San Francisco, people say it all the time—the Chinese are taking over the city.

During the Gold Rush, in the mid-nineteenth century, Chinese miners were chased off the fields by other prospectors. Mexicans (many of whom arrived from northern Mexico, bringing with them mining skills) were also chased away. But many generations later, now, the parent in Walnut Creek, a father of three, tells me that Asians are unfair. (His daughter has not been admitted to Berkeley.) "Asians are unfair because they work so hard."

In the 1970s, when L.A. officials boasted that their city was "the Pacific Rim capital," it seemed easy. After all, no one at the Chamber of Commerce imagined the Pacific Rim might also include the countries of Latin America. And no one imagined that the term had anything to do with freighters sagging with Chinese immigrants, eager for jobs at downtown sweatshops. L.A.—the Pacific Rim capital . . . Californians imagined that the providence of God that had created this lovely place would fulfill itself. We would be able to live off the fat of the emerging global economy, and we would pay no price.

The century that began with the European invention of passports is ending with international airline fares that even a peasant can manage. Fax machines and television made the isolation of China during the Tiananmen Square demonstrations impossible. Movies and jet airplanes are making California alluring in the tiniest villages of Asia and Latin America.

The most modern people I meet in 1993 are alternately those international businessmen who fly business class and deal with several currencies, and those peasants who fly tourist class or crawl or float or walk into the United States. What the migrant worker and the international business executive understand is the inevitable free flow of cash and labor around the modern world.

Senator Dianne Feinstein wonders if we shouldn't charge a toll for entering California from Mexico. And her fellow liberal in the Senate, Barbara Boxer, wants to enlist the National Guard to protect our border. But, of course, millions of middle-class Californians assume that they can use Mexico whenever and however they want. They go to Mexico for a tan. They go to Mexico to adopt a baby. They retire to Mexico—get a condo in Cabo. They reach into Mexico for an inexpensive gardener or nanny.

Despite ourselves and because of the immigrants, California is becoming a world society—an extraordinary meeting place of Asia and Latin America with white and black America.

Poor New York, thousands of miles away, senses that something is going on in California but hasn't a clue. All summer, New York has been taken by the notion that the California dream is tarnished. The *New Yorker* dispatched Joan Didion from her Upper East Side apartment. Regis Philbin confided to his viewers: "It's so sad—all those poor people going to L.A."

CBS News sent several correspondents to Los Angeles a few weeks ago to view the apocalypse. Except for an eccentric Latino who predicted a Latino takeover of the Southland, the entire hour of "48 Hours" was given to white and black opinions. Lots of blond people said they were fed up with California—"It's not what we had in mind." No correspondent bothered to ask the Guatemalan teenager or the Chinese short-order cook why they had come to California.

Dear Regis Philbin: California does not have an immigrant problem. California has a native-born problem. I worry more about the third-generation Mexican American in Boyle Heights than about the newly arrived Mexican immigrant.

Governor Wilson, I think, would have done better addressing a letter to his fellow Californians—rich, middle-class, poor. The governor might well have asked if, as Californians, we assume too much about our right to leisure, and the government's obligation to our well-being.

Ross Perot may have it half right. Americans are going to have to be harder on ourselves. The government is running out of money for savings-and-loan fat cats, Social Security grandmas, and welfare mothers. But Perot is wrong in thinking that we can close ourselves from the world.

Neighbors should not live oblivious of one another. Any coyote in Tijuana will tell you that illegal immigration is inevitable as long as distinctions between rich countries and poor, developed countries and the Third World are not ameliorated. If we want fewer illegal Mexican immigrants, we must work with Mexico, as Mexico must work with Guatemala.

So much nonsense has lately been written about the resistance of the new immigrants to America. UCLA undergraduates and Harvard professors propose multiculturalism in the name of the new immigrants. The truth is that, in time, California will turn the Mexican and Chinese teenagers into rock stars and surfers. But I think the immigrants also will change California—their gift to us—reminding us of what our German and Italian ancestors knew when they came, hopeful, to the brick tenement blocks of the East Coast. Life is work.

IV. A Shared Culture?

Immigrants and Family Values
Francis Fukuyama

Francis Fukuyama is resident consultant at the RAND Corporation in Washington, D.C., and the author of *The End of History and the Last Man*. "Immigrants and Family Values" first appeared in *Commentary*, May 1993.

AT THE REPUBLICAN National Convention in Houston in August 1992, Patrick J. Buchanan announced the coming of a block-by-block war to "take back our culture." Buchanan is right that a cultural war is upon us, and that this fight will be a central American preoccupation now that the Cold War is over. What he understands less well, however, is that the vast majority of the non-European immigrants who have come into this country in the past couple of decades are not the enemy. Indeed, many of them are potentially on his side.

Conservatives have for long been sharply divided on the question of immigration. Many employers and proponents of free-market economics, like Julian Simon or the editorial page of the *Wall Street Journal,* are strongly pro-immigration; they argue for open borders because immigrants are a source of cheap labor and ultimately create more wealth than they consume. Buchanan and other traditional right-wing Republicans, by contrast, represent an older nativist position. They dispute the economic benefits of immigration, but more importantly look upon immigrants as bearers of foreign and less desirable cultural values. It is this group of conservatives who forced the inclusion of a plank in the Republican platform in 1992 calling for the creation of "structures" to maintain the integrity of America's southern border.

Indeed, hostility to immigration has made for peculiar bedfellows. The Clinton administration's difficulties in finding an attorney general who had not at some point hired an illegal-immigrant babysitter is testimony to the objective dependence of liberal yuppies on immigration to maintain their lifestyles, and they by and large would support the *Wall Street Journal*'s open-borders position.

On the other hand, several parts of the liberal coalition—blacks and environmentalists—have been increasingly vocal in recent years in opposition to further immigration, particularly from Latin America. The Black Leadership Forum, headed by Coretta Scott King and Congressman Walter Fauntroy, has lobbied to maintain sanctions against employers hiring illegal immigrant labor on the ground that this takes away jobs from blacks and "legal" browns. Jack Miles, a former *Los Angeles Times* book-review editor with impeccable liberal credentials, has in an article in the *Atlantic* lined up with the Federation for American Immigration Reform (FAIR) in calling for a rethinking of open borders, while liberal activist groups like the Southern California Interfaith Taskforce on Central America have supported Senator Orrin Hatch's legislation strengthening employer sanctions. Environmental groups like the Sierra Club, for their part, oppose immigration because it necessitates economic growth, use of natural resources, and therefore environmental degradation.

But if much of the liberal opposition to immigration has focused on economic issues, the conservative opposition has concentrated on the deeper cultural question; and here the arguments made by the right are very confused. The symptoms of cultural decay are all around us, but the last people in the world we should be blaming are recent immigrants.

•   •   •

The most articulate and reasoned recent conservative attack on immigration came in the summer of 1992 in an article in *National Review* by Peter Brimelow. Brimelow, a senior editor at *Forbes* and himself a naturalized American of British and Canadian background, argues that immigration worked in the past in America only because earlier waves of nativist backlash succeeded in limiting it to a level that could be successfully assimilated into the dominant Anglo-Saxon American culture. Brimelow criticizes pro-immigration free-marketeers like Julian Simon for ignoring the issue of the skill levels of the immigrant labor force, and their likely impact on blacks and others at the bottom end of the economic ladder. But his basic complaint is a cultural one. Attacking the *Wall Street Journal*'s Paul Gigot for remarking that a million Zulus would probably work harder than a million Englishmen today, Brimelow notes:

> This comment reveals an utter innocence about the reality of ethnic and cultural differences, let alone little things like tradition and history—in short, the greater part of the conservative vision. Even in its own purblind terms, it is totally false. All the empirical evidence is that immigrants from developed countries assimilate better than those from underdeveloped countries. It is developed countries that teach the skills required for success in the United States . . . it should not be necessary to explain that the legacy of [the Zulu kings] Shaka and Cetewayo—overthrown just over a century ago—is not that of Alfred the Great, let alone Elizabeth II or any civilized society.

Elsewhere, Brimelow suggests that culture is a key determinant of economic performance, and that people from certain cultures are therefore likely to do less well economically than others. He implies, furthermore, that some immigrants are more prone to random street crime because of their "impulsiveness and present-orientation," while others are responsible for organized crime that is, by his account, ethnically based. Finally, Brimelow argues that the arrival of diverse non-European cultures fosters the present atmosphere of multiculturalism, and is, to boot, bad for the electoral prospects of the Republican Party.

A similar line of thought runs through Buchanan's writings and speeches, and leads to a similar anti-immigrant posture. Buchanan has explicitly attacked the notion that democracy represents a particularly positive form of government, and hence would deny that belief in universal democratic principles ought to be at the core of the American national identity. But if one subtracts democracy from American nationality, what is left? Apparently, though Buchanan is somewhat less explicit on this point, a concept of America as a Christian, ethnically European nation with certain core cultural values that are threatened by those coming from other cultures and civilizations.

There is an easy, Civics 101–type answer to the Brimelow-Buchanan argument. In contrast to other West European democracies, or Japan, the American national identity has never been directly linked to ethnicity or religion. Nationality has been based instead on universal concepts like freedom and equality that are in theory open to all people. Our Constitution forbids the establishment of religion, and the legal system has traditionally held ethnicity at arm's length. To be an American has meant to be committed to a certain set of ideas, and not to be descended from an original tribe of *ur*-Americans. Those elements of a common American culture visible today—belief in the Constitution and the individualist-egalitarian principles underlying it, plus modern American pop and consumer culture—are universally accessible and appealing, making the United States, in Ben Wattenberg's phrase, the first "universal nation."

This argument is correct as far as it goes, but there is a serious counterargument that reaches to the core of last year's debate over "family values." It runs as follows:

America began living up to its universalist principles only

in the last half of this century. For most of the period from its revolutionary founding to its rise as a great, modern, industrial power, the nation's elites conceived of the country not just as a democracy based on universal principles, but also as a Christian, Anglo-Saxon nation.

American democracy—the counterargument continues—is, of course, embodied in the laws and institutions of the country, and will be imbibed by anyone who learns to play by its rules. But virtually every serious theorist of American democracy has noted that its success depended heavily on the presence of certain predemocratic values or cultural characteristics that were neither officially sanctioned nor embodied in law. If the Declaration of Independence and the Constitution were the basis of America's *Gesellschaft* (society), Christian Anglo-Saxon culture constituted its *Gemeinschaft* (community).

Indeed—the counterargument goes on—the civic institutions that Tocqueville observed in the 1830s, whose strength and vitality he saw as a critical manifestation of the Americans' "art of associating," were more often than not of a religious (i.e., Christian) nature, devoted to temperance, moral education of the young, or the abolition of slavery. Nothing in the Constitution states that parents should make large sacrifices for their children, that workers should rise early in the morning and labor long hours in order to get ahead, that people should emulate rather than undermine their neighbors' success, that they should be innovative, entrepreneurial, or open to technological change. Yet Americans, formed by a Christian culture, possessed these traits in abundance for much of their history, and the country's economic prosperity and social cohesion arguably rested on them.

It is this sort of consideration that underlay the family-values controversy during the 1992 election. Basic to this line of thought is that, all other things being equal, children are better off when raised in stable, two-parent, heterosexual families. Such family structures and the web of moral obligations they entail are the foundation of educational achievement, economic success, good citizenship, personal character, and a host of other social virtues.

The issue of family values was badly mishandled by the Republicans and deliberately misconstrued by the press and the Democrats (often not distinguishable), such that mere mention of the phrase provoked derisive charges of narrow-minded gay-bashing and hostility to single mothers. Yet while many Americans did not sign on to last year's family-values theme, few would deny that the family and community are in deep crisis today. The breakdown of the black family in inner-city neighborhoods around America in the past couple of generations shows in particularly stark form the societal consequences of a loss of certain cultural values. And what has happened among blacks is only an extreme extension of a process that has been proceeding apace among whites as well.

The issue, then, is not whether the questions of culture and cultural values are important, or whether it is legitimate to raise them, but whether immigration really threatens those values. For while the values one might deem central either to economic success or to social cohesion may have arisen out of a Christian, Anglo-Saxon culture, it is clear that they are not bound to that particular social group: some groups, like Jews and Asians, might come to possess these values in abundance, while Wasps themselves might lose them and decay. The question thus becomes: which ethnic groups in today's America are threatening, and which groups are promoting, these core cultural values?

•   •   •

The notion that non-European immigrants are a threat to family values and other core American cultural characteristics is, in a way, quite puzzling. After all, the breakdown of traditional family structures, from extended to nuclear, has long been understood to be a disease of advanced industrial countries and not of nations just emerging from their agricultural pasts.

Some conservatives tend to see the Third World as a vast, global underclass, teeming with the same social pathologies as Compton in Los Angeles or Bedford-Stuyvesant in Brooklyn. But the sad fact is that the decay of basic social relationships evident in American inner cities, stretching to the most intimate moral bonds linking parents and children, may well be something with few precedents in human history. Economic conditions in most Third World countries simply would not permit a social group suffering so total a collapse of family structure to survive: with absent fathers and no source of income, or mothers addicted to drugs, children would not live to adulthood.

But it would also seem *a priori* likely that Third World immigrants should have stronger family values than white, middle-class, suburban Americans, while their work ethic and willingness to defer to traditional sources of authority would be greater as well. Few of the factors that have led to family breakdown in the American middle class over the past couple of generations—rapidly changing economic conditions, with their attendant social disruptions; the rise of feminism and the refusal of women to play traditional social roles; or the legitimization of alternative lifestyles and consequent proliferation of rights and entitlements on a retail level—apply in Third World situations. Immigrants coming from traditional developing societies are likely to be poorer, less educated, and in possession of fewer skills than those from Europe, but they are also likely to have stronger family structures and moral inhibitions. Moreover, despite the greater ease of moving to America today than in the last century, immigrants are likely to be a self-selecting group with a much-greater-than-average degree of energy, ambition, toughness, and adaptability.

These intuitions are largely borne out by the available empirical data, particularly if one disaggregates the different parts of the immigrant community.

The strength of traditional family values is most evident among immigrants from East and South Asia, where mutually supportive family structures have long been credited as the basis for their economic success. According to Census Bureau statistics, 78 percent of Asian and Pacific Islander households in the United States were family households, as opposed to 70 percent for white Americans. The sizes of these family households is likely to be larger: 74 percent consist of three or more persons, compared to 57 percent for white families. While Asians are equally as likely to be married as whites, they are only half as likely to be divorced. Though dropping off substantially in the second and third generations, concern for elderly parents is high in Chinese, Japanese, and Vietnamese households for many, and the thought of sticking a mother or father out of sight and out of mind in a nursing home continues to be anathema. More importantly, most of the major Asian immigrant groups are intent on rapid assimilation into the American mainstream, and have not been particularly vocal in pressing for particularistic cultural entitlements.

While most white Americans are ready to recognize and celebrate the social strengths of Asians, the real fears of cultural invasion surround Latinos. Despite their fast growth, Asians still constitute less than 3 percent of the U.S. population, while the number of Hispanics increased from 14.6 to over 22 million between 1980 and 1990, or 9 percent of the population. But here as well, the evidence suggests that most Latin American immigrants may be a source of strength with regard to family values, and not a liability.

Latinos today constitute an extremely diverse group. It is certainly the case that a segment of the Latino community has experienced many of the same social problems as blacks. This is particularly true of the first large Latino community in the United States: Puerto Ricans who came to the mainland in the early postwar period and settled predominantly in New York and other cities of the Northeast. Forty percent of Puerto Rican families are headed by women, compared to 16 percent for the non-Hispanic population; only 57 percent of Puerto Rican households consist of families, while their rate of out-of-wedlock births is almost double the rate for non-Hispanics. In New York, Puerto Ricans have reexported social pathologies like crack-cocaine use to Puerto Rico over the past generation.

Other Latino groups have also brought social problems with them: the Mariel boat lift from Cuba, during which Castro emptied his country's jails and insane asylums, had a measurable impact on crime in the United States. Many war-hardened immigrants from El Salvador and other unstable Central American countries have contributed to crime in the United States, and Chicano gangs in Los Angeles and other southwestern cities have achieved their own notoriety beside the black Bloods and Crips. Half of those arrested in the Los Angeles riot last year were Latinos.

Such facts are highly visible and contribute to the impression among white Americans that Latinos as a whole have joined inner-city blacks to form one vast, threatening underclass. But there are very significant differences among Latino groups. Latinos of Cuban and Mexican origin, for example, who together constitute 65 percent of the Hispanic community, have a 50 percent lower rate of female-headed households than do Puerto Ricans—18.9 and 19.6 percent versus 38.9 percent. While the rate of Puerto Rican out-of-wedlock births approaches that of blacks (53.0 versus 63.1 percent of live births), the rates for Cuban and Mexican-origin Latinos are much lower, 16.1 and 28.9 percent, respectively, though they are still above the white rate of 13.9 percent.

When looked at in the aggregate, Latino family structure stands somewhere between that of whites and blacks. For example, the rates of female-headed families with no husband present as a proportion of total families is 13.5 percent for whites, 46.4 percent for blacks, and 24.4 percent for Hispanics. If we adjust these figures for income level, however, Hispanics turn out to be much closer to the white norm.

Poverty is hard on families regardless of race; part of the reason for the higher percentage of Latino female-headed households is simply that there are more poor Latino families. If we compare families below the poverty level, the Hispanic rate of female-headed families is very close to that of whites (45.7 versus 43.6 percent), while the comparable rate for blacks is much higher than either (78.3 percent). Considering the substantially higher rate of family breakdown within the sizable Puerto Rican community, this suggests that the rate of single-parent families for Cuban- and Mexican-origin Latinos is actually lower than that for whites at a comparable income level.

Moreover, Latinos as a group are somewhat more likely to be members of families than either whites or blacks. Another study indicates that Mexican-Americans have better family demographics than do whites, with higher birthweight babies even among low-income mothers due to taboos on smoking, drinking, and drug use during pregnancy. Many Latinos remain devout Catholics, and the rate of church attendance is higher in the Mexican community than for the United States as a whole as well. But even if one does not believe that the United States is a "Christian country," the fact that so many immigrants are from Catholic Latin America should make them far easier to assimilate than, say, Muslims in Europe.

These statistics are broadly in accord with the observations of anyone who has lived in Los Angeles, San Diego, or any other community in the American Southwest. Virtually every early-morning commuter in Los Angeles knows the street corners on which Chicano day-laborers gather at 7:00 A.M., looking for work as gardeners, busboys, or on construction sites. Many of them are illegal immigrants with families back in Mexico to whom they send their earnings. While they are poor and unskilled, they have a work ethic and devotion to family comparable to those of the South and East European immigrants who came to the United States at the turn of the century. It is much less common to see African-Americans doing this sort of thing.

Those who fear Third World immigration as a threat to Anglo-American cultural values do not seem to have noticed what the real sources of cultural breakdown have been. To some extent, they can be traced to broad socioeconomic factors over which none of us has control: the fluid, socially disruptive nature of capitalism; technological change; economic pressures of the contemporary workplace and urban life and so on. But the ideological assault on traditional family values—the sexual revolution; feminism and the delegitimization of the male-dominated household; the celebration of alternative lifestyles; attempts ruthlessly to secularize all aspects of American public life; the acceptance of no-fault divorce and the consequent rise of single-parent households—was not the creation of recently arrived Chicano agricultural workers or Haitian boat people, much less of Chinese or Korean immigrants. They originated right in the heart of America's well-established white, Anglo-Saxon community. The "Hollywood elite" who create the now-celebrated Murphy Brown, much like the establishment of "media elite" that Republicans enjoy attacking, do not represent either the values or the interests of most recent Third World immigrants.

In short, though the old, traditional culture continues to exist in the United States, it is overlaid today with an elite culture that espouses very different values. The real danger is not that these elites will become corrupted by the habits and practices of Third World immigrants, but rather that the immigrants will become corrupted by them. And that is in fact what tends to happen.

While the first generation of immigrants to the United

States tends to be deferential to established authority and preoccupied with the economic problems of "making it," their children and grandchildren become aware of their own entitlements and rights, more politicized, and able to exploit the political system to defend and expand those entitlements. While the first generation is willing to work quietly at minimum- or subminimum-wage jobs, the second and third generations have higher expectations as to what their labor is worth. The extension of welfare and other social benefits to noncitizens through a series of court decisions has had the perverse effect of hastening the spread of welfare dependency. Part of the reason that Puerto Ricans do less well than other Latino groups may be that they were never really immigrants at all, but U.S. citizens, and therefore eligible for social benefits at a very early stage.

As Julian Simon has shown, neither the absolute nor the relative levels of immigration over the past decade have been inordinately high by historical standards. What *is* different and very troubling about immigration in the present period is that the ideology that existed at the turn of the century and promoted assimilation into the dominant Anglo-Saxon culture has been replaced by a multicultural one that legitimates and even promotes continuing cultural differentness.

The intellectual and social origins of multiculturalism are complex, but one thing is clear: it is both a Western and an American invention. The American founding was based on certain Enlightenment notions of the universality of human equality and freedom, but such ideas have been under attack within the Western tradition itself for much of the past two centuries. The second half of the late Allan Bloom's *The Closing of the American Mind* (the part that most buyers of the book skipped over) chronicles the way in which the relativist ideas of Nietzsche and Heidegger were transported to American shores at mid-century. Combined with an easygoing American egalitarianism, they led not just to a belief in the need for cultural tolerance, but to a positive assertion of the equal moral validity of all cultures. Today the writings of Michel Foucault, a French epigone of Nietzsche, have become the highbrow source of academic multiculturalism.

France may have produced Foucault, but France has not implemented a multicultural educational curriculum to anything like the degree the United States has. The origins of multiculturalism here must therefore be traced to the specific circumstances of American social life. Contrary to the arguments of multiculturalism's promoters, it was not a necessary adjustment to the reality of our pluralistic society. The New York City public school system in the year 1910 was as diverse as it is today, and yet it never occurred to anyone to celebrate and preserve the native cultures of the city's Italians, Greeks, Poles, Jews, or Chinese.

The shift in attitudes toward cultural diversity can be traced to the aftermath of the civil rights movement, when it became clear that integration was not working for blacks. The failure to assimilate was interpreted as an indictment of the old, traditional mainstream Anglo-Saxon culture: "Wasp" took on a pejorative connotation, and African Americans began to take pride in the separateness of their own traditions. Ironically, the experience of African Americans became the model for subsequent immigrant groups like Latinos who could have integrated themselves into mainstream society as easily as the Italians or Poles before them.

It is true that Hispanic organizations now constitute part of the multiculturalist coalition and have been very vocal in pushing for bilingual/bicultural education. There is increasing evidence, however, that rank-and-file immigrants are much more traditionally assimilationist than some of their more vocal leaders. For example, most Chinese and Russian immigrant parents in New York City deliberately avoid sending their children to the bilingual-education classes offered to them by the public school system, believing that a cold plunge into English will be a much more effective means of learning to function in American society.

Hispanics generally show more support for bilingual education, but even here a revealing recent study indicates that an overwhelming number of Hispanic parents see bilingualism primarily as a means of learning English, and not of preserving Hispanic culture. This same study indicates that most Hispanics identify strongly with the United States, and show a relatively low level of Spanish maintenance in the home. By contrast, multiculturalism is more strongly supported by many other groups—blacks, feminists, gays, Native Americans, etc.—whose ancestors have been in the country from the start.

Brimelow's *National Review* piece suggests that even if immigrants are not responsible for our antiassimilationist multiculturalism, we need not pour oil on burning waters by letting in more immigrants from non-Western cultures. But this argument can be reversed: even if the rate of new immigration fell to zero tomorrow, and the most recent five million immigrants were sent home, we would still have an enormous problem in this country with the breakdown of a core culture and the infatuation of the school system with trendy multiculturalist educational policies.

The real fight, the central fight, then, should not be over keeping newcomers out: this will be a waste of time and energy. The real fight ought to be over the question of assimilation itself: whether we believe that there is enough to our Western, rational, egalitarian, democratic civilization to force those coming to the country to absorb its language and rules, or whether we carry respect for other cultures to the point that Americans no longer have a common voice with which to speak to one another.

Apart from the humble habits of work and family values, opponents of immigration ought to consider culture at the high end of the scale. As anyone who has walked around an elite American university recently would know, immigration from Asia is transforming the nature of American education. For a country that has long prided itself on technological superiority, and whose whole economic future rests in large part on a continuing technical edge, a depressingly small number of white Americans from long-established families choose to go into engineering and science programs in preference to business and, above all, law school. (This is particularly true of the most dynamic and vocal part of the white population, upwardly mobile middle-class women.) The one bright spot in an otherwise uniform horizon of decline in educational test scores has been in math, where large numbers of new Asian test-takers have bumped up the numbers. In Silicon Valley alone, there are some 12,000 engineers of Chinese descent, while Chinese account for two out of every five engineering and science graduates in the University of California system.

Indeed, if one were to opt for "designer immigration" that would open the gates to peoples with the best cultural values, it is not at all clear that certain European countries would end up on top.

In the past decade, England's per-capita GNP has fallen behind Italy's, and threatens to displace Portugal and Greece at the bottom of the European Community heap by the end of the decade. Only a fifth of English young people receive any form of higher education, and despite Margaret Thatcher's best efforts, little progress has been made over the past generation in breaking down the stifling social rigidities of the British class system. The English working class is among the least well-educated, most state- and welfare-dependent and immobile of any in the developed world. While the British intelligentsia and upper classes continue to intimidate middle-class Americans, they can do so only on the basis of snobbery and inherited but rapidly dwindling intellectual capital. Paul Gigot may or may not be right that a million Zulus would work harder than a million

English, but a million Taiwanese certainly would, and would bring with them much stronger family structures and entrepreneurship to boot.

•   •   •

This is not to say that immigration will not be the source of major economic and social problems for the United States in the future. There are at least three areas of particular concern.

The first has to do with the effects of immigration on income distribution, particularly at the low end of the scale. The growing inequality of American income distribution over the past decade is not, as the Democrats asserted during the election campaign, the result of Reagan-Bush tax policies or the failure of "trickle-down" economics. Rather, it proceeds from the globalization of the American economy: low-skill labor in Malaysia, Brazil, Mexico, and elsewhere. But it has also had to compete with low-skill immigrant labor coming into the country from the Third World, which explains why Hispanics themselves tend to oppose further Hispanic immigration. The country as a whole may be better off economically as a result of this immigration, but those against whom immigrants directly compete have been hurt, just as they will be hurt by the North American Free Trade Agreement (NAFTA), the General Agreement on Tariffs and Trade (GATT), and other trade-liberalizing measures that are good for the country as a whole. In a city like Los Angeles, Hispanics with their stronger social ties have displaced blacks out of a variety of menial jobs, adding to the woes of an already troubled black community.

The second problem area has to do with the regional concentration of recent Hispanic immigration. As everyone knows, the twenty-five million Hispanics in the United States are not evenly distributed throughout the country, but are concentrated in the Southwest portion of it, where the problems normally accompanying the assimilation of immigrant communities tend to be magnified. The L.A. public school system is currently in a state of breakdown, as it tries to educate burgeoning numbers of recent immigrants on a recession-starved budget.

The third problem concerns bilingualism and the elite Hispanic groups that promote and exist off it. As noted earlier, the rank and file of the Hispanic community seems reasonably committed to assimilation; the same cannot be said for its leadership. Bilingualism, which initially began as a well-intentioned if misguided bridge toward learning English, has become in the eyes of many of its proponents a means of keeping alive a separate Spanish language and culture. Numerous studies have indicated that students in bilingual programs learn English less well than those without access to them, and that their enrollments are swelled by a large number of Hispanics who can already speak English perfectly well. In cities with large Hispanic populations like New York and Los Angeles, the bilingual bureaucracy has become something of a monster, rigidly tracking students despite the wishes of parents and students. The *New York Times* recently reported the case of a Hispanic-surnamed child, born in the United States and speaking only English, who was forced by New York City officials to enroll in an English-as-a-second-language class. Bilingualism is but one symptom of a much broader crisis in American public education, and admittedly makes the problems of assimilation much greater.

These problems can be tackled with specific changes in public policy. But the central issue raised by the immigration question is indeed a cultural one, and as such less susceptible of policy manipulation. The problem here is not the foreign culture that immigrants bring with them from the Third World, but the contemporary elite culture of Americans—Americans like Kevin Costner, who believes that America began going downhill when the white man set foot here, or another American, Ice-T, whose family has probably been in the country longer than Costner's and who believes that women are bitches and that the chief enemy of his generation is the police. In the upcoming block-by-block cultural war, the enemy will not speak Spanish or have a brown skin. In Pogo's words, "He is us."

The Forbidden Topic
Lawrence Auster

Lawrence Auster is the author of *The Path to National Suicide: An Essay on Immigration and Multiculturalism.* "The Forbidden Topic" first appeared in *National Review,* April 27, 1992.

ACROSS THE COUNTRY, America's mainstream identity is being dismantled in the name of "inclusion." Half of New York City's Shakespeare Festival in 1991 was given over to Spanish and Portuguese translations of Shakespeare. Christmas has been replaced in many schools by a nondenominational Winterfest or by the new African-American holiday Kwanza, while schools in areas with large Hispanic populations celebrate Cinco de Mayo. The exemplary figures of American history have been excised from school textbooks, replaced by obscure minorities and women. Despite massive additions of material on non-Western societies, school texts are still being stridently attacked as "Eurocentric," and much more radical changes are in the works.

Yet even as the multiculturalist revolution rolls through the land, there is still profound disagreement about its meaning, its aims, and most of all its origins. Mainstream media and educationists describe the diversity movement as, in part, an effort to be more inclusive of America's historic minorities; in its larger dimensions, however, they see it as a response to the prodigious changes that are occurring in America's ethnic composition. America is rapidly becoming multiracial and white-minority, and, these observers say, our national identity is changing in response. If that is true—and it is stated or implied in almost every news story on the subject—then it is also true that the massive Third World immigration of recent years, the principal source of America's shifting demographics, is itself the ultimate driving force behind multiculturalism.

Virtually alone in resisting these assumptions is the conservative establishment, particularly the neoconservatives. Liberals, who *support* both unrestricted immigration and multiculturalism, do not hesitate to point out a causal link between the two; indeed, they appeal to the inevitability of continued Third World immigration as an unanswerable argument for multiculturalism. Traditional conservatives like Patrick Buchanan, who with equal consistency *oppose* both multiculturalism and Third World immigration, also have no difficulty in seeing the causal connection. Neoconservatives, by contrast, have dissociated these two issues, leading the fight against multiculturalism while passionately clinging to the ideal of unrestricted immigration. Their pro-immigration stand, based on a conviction of both its economic necessity and its political morality, compels them to ignore—or ritually dismiss—the mounting evidence that the sea change in America's ethnic identity is fueling the cultural-diversity movement. To keep immigration from coming under attack, they are forced to hunt for alternative explanations for multiculturalism.

This approach was brought into focus in 1991 in articles by Irving Kristol in the *Wall Street Journal,* by Nathan Glazer in the *New Republic,* and by Midge Decter in *Commentary.* Despite wide differences on the effects of multiculturalism (Kristol thinks it's a threat to the West equal to Nazism and Stalinism; Glazer thinks it's no big deal), they reached startlingly similar conclusions about its causes.

Multiculturalism, they argued, has essentially nothing to do with America's increasing ethnic diversity; at bottom it is a desperate, misguided attempt to overcome black educational deficiencies—an effort that radicals have opportunistically seized upon to advance their separatist and anti-West agenda. "Did these black students and their problems not exist, we would hear little of multiculturalism," Irving Kristol declared. Assimilation, he believes, is proceeding apace: "Most Hispanics are behaving very much like the Italians of yesteryear; most Orientals, like the Jews of yesteryear." Nathan Glazer agreed: "[I]t is not the new immigration that is driving the multicultural demands."

Down with Eurocentrism

Ironically, on the same day Irving Kristol was denying that Hispanics are pushing for multiculturalism, the *New York Times* ran this typical item: "Buoyed by a growing population and by a greater pressure on local school boards, Hispanic Americans have begun pressing textbook publishers and state education officials to include more about Hispanic contributions in the curriculums of public schools," as well as to correct "stereotypes"—a familiar code for the elimination of Eurocentrism.

A spate of letters to the *Wall Street Journal* protesting Kristol's view offered a revealing glimpse into mainstream opinion on the subject. The chief factor in multiculturalism, wrote Martha Farnsworth Riche of the Population Reference Bureau, is that "racially and ethnically, America's school-age population is increasingly unlike its past generations. . . . This ensures that the school-age population will become even less a product of what we call 'Western civilization' in the future." Multiculturalism, said another correspondent, "is not an attempt to address the social problems of African Americans. Latin Americans and Asian Americans have been equally involved." From the cultural left, Gregory K. Tanaka said that as a result of the increasing proportion of nonwhites in America, "it is becoming clear that our Western 'common' culture no longer works. What Mr. Kristol overlooks is that this decline of Westernism leaves us no surviving basis for social order."

While it might be tempting to dismiss these views as multiculturalist propaganda, the clincher is that Nathan Glazer himself, after at first denying that the increase of non-European groups is propelling multiculturalism, turned around and admitted it: "I do not see how school systems with a majority of black *and Latino* students, with black *or Latino* leadership at the top . . . can stand firmly against the multiculturalist thrust . . . *demographic and political pressures change the history that is to be taught.*" (Italics added.) It was in this same article that Glazer, to the great consternation of his neoconservative allies, announced his reluctant support for Thomas Sobol's radical multicultural curriculum reforms in New York State. That Glazer subscribed to the demographics-multiculturalism link in the very act of surrendering to the new multicultural curriculum supports my point that once multiculturalism is accepted, the key role of immigration and ethnic diversity in driving multiculturalism loses its stigma and can be freely acknowledged.

To this, conservatives reply that Glazer is not admitting a forbidden truth but is simply adopting the multiculturalists' fallacious "demographic inevitability" argument. In *The New Criterion,* Heather MacDonald agrees that demographic changes are "fueling" multiculturalism, but criticizes Glazer for "[mistaking] the actual for the inevitable." In other words, neoconservatives will concede that multiculturalism has been adopted because of our society's increasing diversity; but, they insist, this was not "logical." Since immigration is only the "actual" cause and not the "logical" cause, we should leave immigration alone.

One can't help but be reminded of the people who say that the failures of Marxism do not prove its *theoretical* unsoundness. Just as one cannot persuade a devoted Marxist that Marxism must lead to tyranny and poverty, one cannot logically demonstrate to an open-borders conservative that precipitately changing an historically European-majority country into a multiracial, white-minority country must result in a breakdown of the common culture. Nevertheless, whether logical or not, that is what is happening.

Here neoconservatives fall back on the familiar argument that it is only the ethnic activists, not the great mass of the immigrant groups, who are pushing for multiculturalism, a case advanced most recently by Linda Chavez in *Out of the Barrio*. But as Tamar Jacoby has pointed out in a perceptive review, Miss Chavez's own evidence suggests quite the opposite conclusion: that Hispanics of all classes are eagerly embracing the call to cultural separatism. According to one study cited by Miss Chavez, a large and rising percentage of Hispanics describe themselves as "Hispanic first/American second"—a preference made clear by the Hispanic majority in San Jose, California, who angrily protested, as a "symbol of conquest," a statue commemorating the raising of the American flag in California during the Mexican War.

But even if it were true that most of the new ethnics didn't "want" multiculturalism, it is undeniable that their swelling numbers empower the group-rights movement by adding to its clientele. As soon as minority immigrants arrive in this country, they become grist for the affirmative-action mill, eligible for an elaborate web of racial preferences. To imagine that we can turn back the multiculturalist and group-rights ideology by persuasion alone, while continuing the large-scale immigration that feeds that ideology, is like forcibly pouring liquor down a man's throat while "advising" him to stay sober.

Apart from ideology, it is important to understand that massive deculturalization is occurring as a direct result of the demographic changes themselves. Commenting on the impact of the huge Hispanic presence in California, an Hispanic academic tells the *New York Times:* "What is threatened here is intellectual life, the arts, museums, symphonies. How can you talk about preserving open space and establishing museums with a large undereducated underclass?" The program director of the Brooklyn Academy of Music speaks matter-of-factly about the inevitable displacement of Western music as the Academy gears its programs to the cultural interests and traditions of Brooklyn's intensely heterogeneous, Third World population.

Another consequence of this profound population shift is an intensification of white guilt. Since in our emerging multiracial society any all-white grouping is increasingly seen as nonrepresentative (and presumptively "racist"), the same assumption gets insensibly projected onto the past. The resulting loss of sympathetic interest in Western historical figures, lore, and achievements creates a ready audience for the multiculturalist rewriting of history. When we can no longer employ traditional reference points such as "our Western heritage" because a critical number of us are no longer from the West; when we cannot speak of "our Founding Fathers" because the expression is considered racially exclusive; when more and more minorities complain that they can't identify with American history because they "don't see people who look like themselves" in that history, then the only practical way to preserve a simulacrum of common identity is to redefine America as a centerless, multicultural society.

Multiculturalism, in sum, is far more than a radical ideology or misconceived educational reform; it is a *mainstream* phenomenon, a systematic dismantling of America's unitary national identity in response to unprecedented ethnic and racial transformation. Admittedly, immigration reform aimed at stabilizing the country's ethnic composition is no panacea; the debunking of multiculturalism must also continue. But if immigration isn't cut back, the multiculturalist thrust will be simply unstoppable.

What explains the conservatives' refusal to face the demographic dimensions of multiculturalism? Martha Farnsworth Riche believes the reason is psychological: "The older white academics are facing a shift in power. They're denying that reality by saying, in effect, that minorities 'should' assimilate; they don't want to face the fact that their world is disappearing." More to the point, they are evading the uncomfortable necessity of dealing with the racially charged aspects of the immigration issue.

Indeed, the conservatives' greatest reason for not allowing a fundamental debate on immigration is their understandable fear of opening up a forum for racist attitudes. But as the 1991 election in Louisiana suggests, the establishment's refusal to take seriously Middle America's legitimate concerns about cultural displacement only makes it more likely that those concerns will be taken up by extremists. If opposition to racism is not to become a destructive ideological crusade, then racism must be defined according to a norm of racial justice that is rationally achievable in this world. Understood in a nonutopian sense, racial justice means that the majority in a country treats minorities fairly and equally; it does not mean that the majority is required to turn *itself* into a minority. If it does mean the latter, then nation-states, in effect, have no right to preserve their own existence, let alone to control their borders.

The immigration restrictions of the early 1920s, discriminatory though they plainly were (and against the group to which this writer belongs), reduced ethnic hatreds, greatly eased the assimilation of white ethnics, and kept America a culturally unified nation through the mid-twentieth century. The falloff in cheap immigrant labor also encouraged capital-intensive investment and spurred the great middle-class economic expansion of the 1920s. It is ironic, therefore, that our open-borders advocates constantly appeal to the turn-of-the-century immigration as a model for us to follow today, since one of the key reasons the earlier immigration turned out, in retrospect, to be such a remarkable success was that it was *halted*. The same caveat applies even more strongly to our present, uncontrolled influx from the Third World.

Why the World Comes Here
Peggy Noonan

Peggy Noonan is the author of *What I Saw at the Revolution: A Political Life in the Reagan Era*, and *Life, Liberty and the Pursuit of Happiness*. She wrote speeches for Ronald Reagan and George Bush from 1984 to 1989. She was previously a producer and writer at CBS News in New York. "Why the World Comes Here" was originally published in *Reader's Digest*, July 1991.

AMERICA IS EXPERIENCING the biggest influx of immigrants since the great wave that ended in the 1920s, the one that brought the grandparents and great-grandparents of the baby boomers who are now, demographically, America. Here in New York these new immigrants, many of them shopkeepers, run a whole level of the city. It is the level that works.

Recently, I heard from a friend who had been thinking about this historic wave of immigration. The facts of the wave are clear—6.3 million newcomers legally immigrated to the United States from 1980 through 1989, most of them from Asia, Mexico, and the Caribbean. The people I grew up with, the European ethnics, are cresting. It's becoming a new America.

Our way of speaking about all this hasn't kept up, my friend says. "We need to replace 'the melting pot.' People don't know what it means anymore—it's poetry from another age, technology has passed it by—and anyway, it no longer applies. To the extent we ever really melted together, we do so less now."

Allow me to offer a new metaphor from an old family custom. Let's call it "the Sunday stew"—rich, various, and roiling, and all of it held together by a good strong broth. The broth, I say, is what we used to call Americanism—a word I haven't thought of in so long it almost stops me cold. It stops my friend, too: we're surprised to arrive at such an old idea.

This conversation reflects, I think, the growing interest America's longtimers are taking in America's newcomers. Most of us see their coming as good news—immigration is affirmation, proof that we are still what we used to be, a haven for the bold and striving dispossessed. But we're concerned, too, about whether we are absorbing them into the country as successfully as we've done in the past. Which brings us to the old-fashioned idea of Americanism, and how to communicate it.

In many ways, immigrants know what Americanism is better than we do. They've paid us the profoundest compliment by leaving the land of their birth to come and spend their lives with us. And they didn't come here to join nothing, they came to join something—us at our best, us as they imagined us after a million movies and books and reports from relatives. They wanted to be part of our raucous drama, and they wanted the three m's—money, mobility, meritocracy.

Take John Lam, who left Hong Kong when he was seventeen to come to New York City. Mornings he attended high school, afternoons he worked in a factory, and at night he waited tables to help support his parents, brother, and five sisters. The bet paid off. Now Lam, thirty-nine, is one of New York's leading silk importers. He owns factories, warehouses, and restaurants, but his garment businesses alone are worth some $80 million.

Dung Nguyen Le fled Vietnam with her family in 1975 at age nine. They spent weeks on a small, overcrowded fishing vessel, made their way to the Philippines, then Guam, and finally settled in the strange, faraway land they were aiming for—America. You can guess the story from there. Dung learned English, was valedictorian of her Pensacola, Florida, high school class, and became a U.S. citizen. After graduating from college with honors and then from medical school, she began her residency at the Halifax Medical Center in Daytona Beach.

"In my old country, only the privileged few go to medical school," says Dr. Le. "But here in the United States many more opportunities are available to me."

Then there's what might simply be called the American style. For a lot of immigrants, America has a special quality reflected in a comment by a twenty-one-year-old New Zealander I know. "Everything's happening here," she said. "America's just so—cool." Yes, indeed. We are, after all, the kind of people who'd send a volunteer army across the oceans to slam-dunk a dictator, liberate a nation, and leave behind not an army of occupation but soldiers caring for starving refugees. In the 1960s some people accused America of being an imperialist nation; by now it's obvious that the only thing imperialistic about us is our culture, which has swept the world—but only because the world saw our movies and TV shows, loved our blue jeans and posters and fast food, listened to our jukeboxes and begged to be invaded. Deep in its heart the world thinks America is the bravest, sweetest, toughest, funniest place on earth, and for once the world is right.

Which is why the world comes here. And when immigrants arrive, some kind of magic happens: they do extraordinary things, things they couldn't do at home. In Indochina the Asians fight, rent by factionalism; here they build and get dressed up and go to the Westinghouse Awards and Ivy League commencements. In Greece the young are sunk in a funk, with widespread joblessness; here they become entrepreneurs. In Jamaica, people find that just living day to day can be a struggle; here they've raised Colin Powell to become a hero, general, and chairman of the Joint Chiefs of Staff.

Nicholas Barsan grew up in Brasov, Romania, where land ownership was illegal. But in America he made property his trade. Some have called him the world's best real estate salesman. In 1986 he earned $1.1 million by closing nearly ninety deals worth $27 million. Roberto Arguello fled Nicaragua in 1979 when Marxist revolutionaries overthrew the government and shut down his business. Where could he go? He came to America, found a partner, bought a supermarket in the Bronx and then a grocery store in Brooklyn. Today, the two stores gross $22 million a year.

Nationwide, the small shops the immigrants run create thousands of jobs and contribute billions to the economy. In return, the newcomers get the possibility of dreams. But these dreams aren't free. There's a price to pay: once you're here, you have to become Americanized.

We need to communicate to these newcomers the moral and philosophical underpinnings of what they've joined, the things that keep us together. These include the reasons we fought the Revolutionary War and the Civil War, the meaning of the civil rights movement, and the reasons we have sent armies across oceans to liberate other nations. To know what we were is to know who we are.

This is why we must not permit school texts to imply, as some do, that "America was founded by white male Euros who broke from Britain over taxes but retained slaves, and two centuries later the liberation is not complete because racism is still rampant." Such sour revisionism is not helpful. And it omits a salient truth: those seeking justice over the years were lucky enough to be operating in a country that had not only a Constitution, but a conscience, to which an appeal could be made. This is a triumph of idealism that is forever a tribute to the human spirit.

Our laudable eagerness to show openness to other cultures should not become a reason to reject our own culture. Recent immigrants themselves worry about this. An Englishman who has been in America for ten years now summed it up: "It's good to be open, but you don't want diversity to become destruction."

Earlier immigrants arrived in an America that was sure of itself and proud of its great achievements. It spoke one language. The immigrants who came at the turn of the century knew that to join the club, they had to learn the language.

Today's immigrants have joined a country that is less sure of its right to impose its language. The result will likely prove not to be ethnic liberation but ethnic segregation. The fact is, America is an English-speaking country, and it won't help us to communicate with one another if, in the twenty-first century, we become a Tower of Babel.

Immigrants and longtimers alike must realize that America is a special place, something new in history. Margaret Thatcher referred to this in her first major speech after leaving Downing Street. "Americans and Europeans sometimes forget how unique the United States is," she said. "No other nation has been built upon an idea—the idea of liberty. Whether in flight from persecution or poverty, [immigrants] have welcomed American values and opportunities. And America herself has bound them to her with powerful bonds of patriotism and pride."

We are in a profound economic transition, from a nation of car makers and steelworkers to a nation of communications and service workers. We're trying to make a transition from being a great nation to being a different kind of great nation. No other country has asked itself to do that. To succeed, we must draw from our newcomers the toughness and resilience of spirit that have nurtured our America since its birth.

Immigrants have always paid us such a compliment by throwing their lot with us. It might be nice, and a surprise, if now and then longtimers took a moment to say what we ought to say after being complimented: thank you. We might even say, Pull up a seat, you're welcome at the table, there's room and abundance for all.

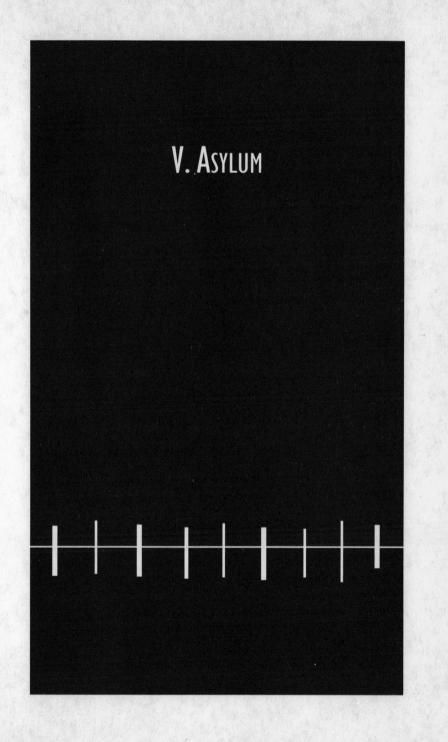

V. Asylum

The United States of Asylum
Ted Conover

Ted Conover is the author of *Coyotes: A Journey Through the Secret World of America's Illegal Aliens.* "The United States of Asylum" first appeared in the *New York Times Magazine,* September 19, 1993.

DONG YISHEN LOOKS a lot better in person than in his lawyer's photo of him. The picture, taken the night of his arrival in Queens on the *Golden Venture,* shows him wearing a thin, ragged blazer and dark turtleneck, his hair still plastered down from the Atlantic Ocean. Now, in the crisp blue uniform of the Salisbury Interim Correctional Facility in Pennsylvania, he looks composed, if a bit nervous.

Fellow prisoners in the visitors' room of the medium-security jail stare as he bows to me and my interpreter. They are in for crimes ranging from burglary to drug offenses. But Dong is a different kind of prisoner—accused not of any crime but of "an administrative violation" of U.S. immigration rules. Technically, he and the other sixty Chinese held at the jail are free to leave—but only for China. And Dong, who is thirty-four, does not want to go back to China.

"In the countryside, if you are a farmer and your first child is a girl the government won't argue too much if you have a second child after five years. But my second one was also a girl. In China we really want to have a son."

Dong and his wife kept trying. To hide from the government, they had their third child in a distant village. It was the long-awaited son. For the first few years, he was raised in the house of childless friends. "But then I admitted that this was my own son—he is now six years old." As a result, says Dong, the authorities, whom he barely eluded, destroyed his furniture and knocked down his house.

Like four other *Golden Venture* survivors I interviewed, Dong is sharp on the details of his persecution but vague about the smugglers. The trip was arranged for him "by friends." He claims he doesn't know exactly how much they paid up front or how much he has to pay off.

One reason for his reticence may be the presence of Chinese "enforcers" in the jail—the Immigration and Naturalization Service suspects that several were on board, and presumes they are mixed in among those imprisoned. He will say that during a horrific storm near the Cape of Good Hope the boat, battered by fifty-foot waves for seven or eight hours, nearly sank.

Though his life has been completely sedentary since he left China's Fujian Province six months ago, he has strong arms, farmer's arms. As we stand up to say good-bye, we shake hands, and Dong will not release his grip. He is shaking my hand with both of his and speaking at me instead of to the interpreter.

"The life I had was not good," he says. "I was so poor. . . . If I'm not allowed to stay, I will have to commit suicide."

It is hard to come face to face with someone in such straits and not feel sympathy. And yet who is to know if he is telling the truth? There is only his word. Dong came here with high hopes. President George Bush, in fact, specifically encouraged this kind of flight in the wake of the 1989 Tiananmen Square killings and pressure from the antiabortion lobby. Dong had reason to think he might qualify for the formal status called political asylum—refuge from political persecution.

But China has nearly 1.2 billion people, more than a fifth of the planet's total; 500 million are of childbearing age. "Is the United States prepared to let them all in?" asks Ling-Chi Wang, associate professor of Asian-American Studies at the University of California at Berkeley. More broadly, in terms of the asylum debate, does Dong's flight from birth control really qualify as political persecution? And if so, is political asylum an ideal that we as a country can still stand behind?

• • •

Skyrocketing asylum applications and the abuse of the system by nefarious figures have brought asylum into the news. Sheik Omar Abdel-Rahman, whose followers are accused of bombing the World Trade Center, has applied for asylum in order to prevent his removal to Egypt. Mir Aimal Kansi, the Pakistani suspected of killing two CIA employees outside their headquarters with an AK-47 early this year, had purchased his weapon using documents obtained with his official work authorization, supplied by the government to most asylum applicants.

Asylum is much in the news because the average citizen lumps it together with all forms of immigration, and in these recession-plagued times, the pendulum is making a swing toward intolerance of immigrants. It is one more component of the fear that we've "lost control of our borders."

In contrast to many European countries, however, asylum here adds only a sliver to overall numbers of immigrants. A hundred thousand people applied for asylum in the last fiscal year (the approval rate is about 30 percent), compared with almost a million who immigrated legally in other government programs.

Notwithstanding recent bad press, asylum, at least in its conception, is a beautiful idea. The notion of granting protection to those fleeing persecution gained strength after World War II from the widespread agreement that what had happened to the Jews would never be allowed to happen again to anybody, anywhere. Countries that signed the United Nations 1951 Convention Relating to Refugees, and its 1967 Protocol, agreed to protect those who met the documents' definition of a refugee: a person with "a well-founded fear of being persecuted for reasons of race, religion, nationality, membership of a particular social group or political opinion." Asylum is offered to refugees who make it to a "safe country" on their own. In the United States, it is administered by the Immigration and Naturalization Service. (The State Department has a separate program that brings over groups of refugees from selected countries.)

World War II also created a world divided into East and West, and asylum, conceived of as ideology-free, soon became an instrument of Cold War politics. Until the collapse of the Soviet Union, asylum was a weapon used to "embarrass our enemies," says Arthur C. Helton, director of the Refugee Project for the Lawyers Committee for Human Rights. Asylees, as they're called—whether ballet dancers, physicists, or fighter pilots—were testimony to the superiority of our system.

The "clear anti-Communist ideology . . . favored only those who appeared to share it," wrote Gil Loesscher and John A. Scanlan in their book *Calculated Kindness: Refugees and America's Half-Open Door, 1945–Present.* "Cubans were the principal beneficiary of this double standard. The Haitians were the principal losers." Eastern Europeans fleeing Communist regimes were practically all approved for asylum; victims of violence in Central American countries that had the support of the U.S. government were routinely denied.

Now that the Cold War is no more, replaced by what might be called the new world disorder, what is going to be acceptable as an evil to flee from?

Fidel Castro may no longer be on the list, as a Cuban airline captain discovered after he diverted his plane to Miami and, along with all but five of the fifty-three people on board, requested political asylum. Instead of granting his request, federal law-enforcement officials, with Cuba's help, pursued criminal charges against the airline captain. This change may reflect not only the thaw in relations with Cuba but also a growing suspicion that asylum applicants, rather than fleeing persecution, are simply seeking entry to the developed world.

Accustomed to measuring dissent from Communism, officials who preside over asylum cases are suddenly faced with a bewildering variety of persecution claims. A homosexual escaping from death squads in Brazil . . . a woman from Africa who does not want to undergo the cruel, potentially crippling procedure called clitoridectomy . . . a Peruvian who has aroused the wrath of the Shining Path . . . A Guatemalan union worker threatened with death for organizing against the government . . . a Christian Sudanese fleeing from Islamic fundamentalists. Many of the world's people, rather than suffer in silence, would prefer to live somewhere else. Like here.

Since millions fear for their lives in many lands, political asylum now raises a much larger immigration question: How many asylees can America take in? And which ones?

•   •   •

People who arrive at Kennedy International Airport without proper papers and apply for asylum are often released, pending their hearings, because of a lack of space at the Wackenhut detention facility, a bleak converted warehouse run by a private company for the immigration service, in Queens, near the airport. Occasionally someone will arrive when one of the 125 beds is empty. Such was the luck of Luis.

Wackenhut, a building intended for goods, not people, has no outdoor exercise yard and practically no windows. Luis, a welder from Peru, has lived ten months under artificial light, leaving the facility only once, for a hearing in

Manhattan. His appeal of an immigration judge's ruling against him was recently turned down.

"I've changed a lot here," says Luis. (His last name is withheld to protect him from persecution should he be returned to Peru.) "I had a big fear of speaking openly, but now less. I want the authorities here to pay attention. The injustice gives me courage. I worry that our cries for justice are being silenced."

Once he begins to talk there is no holding him back. I have seen the slums of Lima and know the place where Luis lives. To see a man like him—bursting with life and moral outrage—come out of that environment is astonishing enough. But to see him in this country and yet not in this country, penned within a block of metal and concrete, fills me with despair.

Luis's story begins in one of the sprawling poor communities known as *pueblos jóvenes* (young towns) on the outskirts of Lima. There he became a leader in a civic group that tried to secure services like electricity and water for the city's half-million people. The group's efforts to help the poor have been recognized by the Pope and the United Nations, but its continuing success has attracted the unwanted attention of Sendero Luminoso, or Shining Path, Peru's violent Maoist guerrilla movement.

"They began to infiltrate our assemblies. We noticed that the ideas being suggested were the ideas of terrorists—that we start an armed struggle. They talked of Communism. But we had never spoken of armed struggle. Our only weapons are work and truth and the faith we have. Seeing that we wouldn't help, the Shining Path started putting on more pressure. Their fliers said that anyone who didn't support the armed struggle was a traitor and would die. But we held firm."

The Shining Path's campaign of intimidation escalated in the late 1980s with the execution of various directors of the group. "One guy they took to a central park and machine-gunned in front of his family. Another time they threw dynamite into a house and many innocents died. They blow up banks, schools, and hospitals. There were 2,000 of us leaders when it began. Many were killed or had to flee. Some of us kept fighting."

Luis says he has "always had the courage to face the bad." But the Shining Path learned that he opposed them from his work counseling teenagers involved with drugs. Soon messages began to be left at his house, telling him to resign his leadership position. His father, in another part of Peru, was also threatened. In a third note delivered to his home, they said they would kill him. Luis, his wife, and three children moved to a safe house.

Fearful for his life and for his family, Luis secured a plane ticket, passport, and false visa from his associates. But in February his application for asylum in the United States was denied by a judge who, noting that Luis had claimed persecution on account of "political opinion," cited a State Department memo on Peru that stated Sendero Luminoso's "choice of victims does not appear to be the result of their personal political views. Rather, the Sendero uses force to intimidate and recruit, to coerce financial support, and to retaliate against those inside and outside the government who are perceived as opposing its goals or undermining its support."

In other words, the Shining Path singled him out for his position, not for his views. But the State Department memo also contradicts itself. If Sendero retaliates against those "who are perceived as opposing its goals," isn't it singling them out for their views? Luis's lawyer appealed, and recently the Board of Immigration Appeals turned him down. Luis's lawyer is appealing again.

Meanwhile, Luis waits in Wackenhut. "I have the hope to return to Peru, to continue my work someday, but I can't right now. I came here to escape the Path."

• • •

I exit Wackenhut, and reenter my privileged position as a citizen of one of the world's prosperous countries, one troubled much less with political ideology, these days, than with the question, mainly, of how much do we share? Are these people our brothers and sisters? And if not, what do we owe a stranger?

"The growth of a global economy has emphasized rather than reduced inequality between nations," says a new report by the United Nations Population Fund, and the number of migrants worldwide is at least 100 million. This migration, away from trouble and poverty and toward peacefulness and opportunity, "could become the human crisis of our age," says the report.

This is not to imply that a hundred million people are packing their bags for America. Gregg A. Beyer, director of asylum for the Immigration and Naturalization Service, uses the example of Latin America to illustrate that most people would probably rather stay home. "From settled countries like Chile and Bolivia, we get very few applications," he notes (sixty and ninety-three, respectively, over a recent ten-month period). "It is the countries in turmoil—like Peru and Colombia—that produce the greatest number" (2,529 and 998, respectively). Beyer's program handles 90 percent of the country's asylum cases—those who apply on their own; the rest—those who are apprehended—fall within the purview of the immigration court.

Still, the numbers are rising rapidly, and if the asylum apparatus is a reflection of the way Americans think about it, it is a subject we find difficult to think about at all. From 1968 to 1975 the United States averaged only two hundred applications per year. The startling rise in applications since—130,000 were expected in 1993—has until recently been met with bureaucratic paralysis. A ballyhooed asylum corps of 150 specially trained officers (Germany has 3,000; Sweden, 800) inherited a backlog of 114,000 cases the day they started work in 1991. There is now a backlog of 300,000 cases.

Those awaiting adjudication are not deportable and, in most cases, are given a work authorization. This means that the backlog itself now attracts spurious claims. Apply for asylum in the United States, it is known, and you can pretty much plan to stay. Depending on where you enter the byzantine process, if you are denied, up to four appeals are possible. Some cases have been pending for twelve years.

But with rising sentiment against immigration and given the notoriety of the recent asylum cases, reform is on the horizon. "We cannot and will not surrender our border to those who wish to exploit our history of compassion and justice," said President Clinton at a White House ceremony in July 1993 announcing a package of immigration reforms.

"Expedited exclusion," which deals with asylum, provides for adjudication within a few days for those arriving at airports without documents and for boat people like Dong Yishen. As the term indicates, the emphasis is on moving people out quickly.

In addition, in September 1993 the President instructed the Immigration and Naturalization Service to come up with new procedures to streamline its unwieldy bureaucracy and to curb its worst abuses. According to Gregg Beyer, these could include a time limit on applying for asylum (there presently is none), a withholding of work authorization from all but those who are granted asylum, and enforcement of the idea of "country of first asylum." Under this last restriction, foreigners who have passed through a country that has a procedure for providing asylum will be returned to that country, if possible.

These reforms—introduced recently in the Senate by Edward M. Kennedy and in the House by Jack Brooks, Democrat from Texas—appear to enjoy broad bipartisan support. But they also have their critics. Warren R. Leiden, executive director of the American Immigration Lawyers Association, notes that if Clinton's "expedited exclusion" becomes law, it will be practically impossible for an airport asylum-seeker to be represented by an attorney, since it takes time to find lawyers, who may need more than a week to prepare their cases. The attorney can make a difference: a 1987 General Accounting Office study noted that applicants with attorneys were three times more likely to succeed in proceedings before an immigration judge.

Lucas Guttentag, director of the Immigrants' Rights Project of the American Civil Liberties Union, worries that the new hurdles will result in bona fide applicants being summarily returned. "Experience has shown that persons who were found by the INS not to have a credible fear initially were later granted asylum under a full hearing," he says. Equally troubling, he adds, is "the absence of judicial review and the attempt to strip the courts of any power to oversee the entire process, because it attempts to insulate the INS from any independent judicial oversight." On many occasions, courts have found the enforcement-minded immigration service to have abridged immigrant rights.

Doubtless one goal of the Clinton reform effort is to send a signal to citizens who fear America has lost control of the borders and to foreign nationals hoping the same thing. But even if the President succeeds in curbing the worst asylum abuses—like the ease in claiming asylum at Kennedy Airport and allowing Chinese claiming persecution under the one-child policy to enter—he will not have touched the underlying shortcomings in the system.

Those applying for asylum upon arriving at an airport or who get caught trying to get in on a boat account for only about 10 percent of the total number of asylum applicants. The rest, who apply once they are in the country (having entered legally on a visa, for example, or illegally across the border), will not be affected by the changes. The backlog continues to grow. And the number of asylum officers remains woefully inadequate.

A congressional staff member who helped frame the Refugee Act of 1980, which gave a real-life commitment to America's symbolic support of refugee protection, recalls that the country was then receiving a little more than 2,000 asylum applications a year. "Let's double it," he said, making a worst-case projection; and Congress foresaw some 5,000 annually. Instead, 26,000 were received the first year.

Unless more money and thought are given this problem, the increase in world refugee numbers will guarantee that America continues its historic pattern of unpreparedness.

• • •

In the basement offices of Central American Legal Assistance in Williamsburg, Brooklyn, I meet Vicente Osorio, his wife, Maria, and their eight-month-old daughter. Of the 300,000 people in the asylum backlog, 154,000 are from either Guatemala or El Salvador—a result of the exodus from those countries in the 1980s and lawsuits that forced the Immigration and Naturalization Service to rehear their cases.

Osorio is a short, round man of strong opinions. A street cleaner, he was on the executive board of a municipal workers' union when it got into a dispute with the Guatemalan government. After the union called a strike that the government termed illegal, seventy-two union members were selectively fired, including Osorio. In response, the union began a long campaign, in the news media and on the streets, to win support for their cause. As the campaign geared up, union members began getting killed or abducted.

"José Mercedes Sotz was beaten, and three months later, as he and his child walked to a bus stop, his child, three years old, was shot and paralyzed," he says. "Other leaders were killed. Some were kidnapped. Others fled. My friend Fufino Reyes, may he rest in peace, died fighting. He was working on a union case at the administration building and he won. Two blocks away from there, after leaving, he was stabbed." (In Osorio's asylum application there are documents from Amnesty International and Americas Watch attesting to this violence.)

Osorio started receiving threats. A man in the office of the municipal government said Osorio should stop his organizing or he would get "disappeared." Written death threats followed, delivered to his home. "I didn't want to leave my wife a widow. Though we were people of bravery and strength, we would only be martyrs if we stayed." The Osorios fled Guatemala, leaving the children with their grandmother. Vicente and María Osorio's fourth child, the eight-month-old, was born in the United States.

The Osorios' initial application for asylum was denied, as was their first appeal. According to immigration officials, "the fundamental nature" of Vicente Osorio's dispute with the Guatemalan government was economic, concerning wages and the reinstatement of workers. "The possible existence of a generalized 'political' motive underlying the government's action is inadequate to establish that the respondent fears persecution on account of political opinion."

The Osorios' lawyer is appealing to a federal appeals court.

●　　●　　●

Exactly what constitutes political persecution?

Sometimes it's hard to tell. Sadruddin Aga Khan, the former United Nations High Commissioner for Refugees, wrote in the *International Herald Tribune* that the identity of refugees has become blurred. Many are "victims of complex socioeconomic and political crises. . . . They may not be pushed out at the end of a rifle or with the threat of execution looming over them, but population pressure, regional conflicts, environmental degradation, and absence of work opportunities combine to encourage if not force them to leave."

In San Francisco in July 1993, probably for the first time in the United States, an immigration judge in San Francisco granted asylum to a homosexual Brazilian fleeing "antigay death squad gangs, who are often joined by the police in their massacres of gays." France recently recognized genital mutilation as a form of persecution in the asylum case of a woman from West Africa. Should these claims be accepted?

Such new directions, says Dan Stein, executive director of the Federation for American Immigration Reform, represent "a backdoor immigration program for people who are displeased and dispossessed, of which there are billions." "When you get into these gray areas where people are fleeing a status"—i.e., a sexual preference—"or a cultural, or an economic repression, you are dealing with the kind of generalized dissatisfaction that our refugee and asylum laws cannot handle, and it's impractical to think they ever could," he says.

The ACLU's Guttentag says Stein "betrays an appalling ignorance" of both the facts and the law and the international standards regarding refugee protection. "The Tenorio decision, if he's read it, reflects a very careful analysis of the actual facts in Brazil, the kinds of threats and attacks to which this person and gay persons in Brazil are actually subjected," says Guttentag. "It was not a person fleeing because of their status. It was a person fleeing because of the discrimination and persecution and the physical threats that that person has specifically suffered."

Though immigration law is based upon benchmark standards like the "well-founded fear of persecution" (echoing language in the United Nations Convention) and guided by the occasional Supreme Court ruling, most precedents are set by the Board of Immigration Appeals, in Falls Church, Va. Some lawyers complain that many of the board's decisions are subjective and increasingly restrictive. "They are defining persecution out of existence," says Anne Pilsbury of Central American Legal Assistance. " 'Persecution' is not an easily definable term," wrote Loescher and Scanlan, "and always derives some of its meaning from the political perspectives of those employing it."

Western Europe has always accepted asylum-seekers in far greater numbers than the United States, but even there the doors are closing. There was a moment following World War II when the world decided that asylum was the right thing to do. It is still the right thing to do. But in the world of the 1990s, Americans are being forced to rethink the implications of that promise.

• • •

At William Ochan's hearing before an immigration judge in Newark, things have suddenly taken a bad turn. Ochan, twenty-nine, is a Christian from southern Sudan. The radical Islamic government of northern Sudan, says Africa Watch, has for nine years waged "a war in the south of extreme brutality" to turn the Sudan into an Islamic state "by whatever means necessary." "The policy has resulted in the suppression of all forms of civil society, the arrest, detention, and torture of dissidents, and the relocation and deprivation of hundreds of thousands of people."

One of the displaced, according to his own testimony, is William Ochan.

He became a refugee, he says, the year he was born; his parents, fearing oppression by Muslims, fled with their children to Uganda. After a truce, he returned to the Sudan at age eleven to live with his grandfather, a pastor and headmaster. While his brother joined the Sudanese People's Liberation Army, the armed Christian guerrilla resistance, William Ochan opted for peaceful resistance. Still, the demonstrations he led landed him in jail in Juba, where during his interrogation soldiers hung him by cords tied to his fingers. His left middle finger was mangled as a result. He shows it to the judge, who describes it for the record. She seems moved by his testimony.

Ochan's application is also supported by a dean's-list record at two New Jersey colleges (he supported himself with two full-time jobs while studying), active participation in church, and an op-ed piece he wrote on the Sudan's crisis that was published in the *Los Angeles Times*. His lawyer has even brought a video of Ochan being interviewed by Charles Kuralt.

But now the Immigration and Naturalization Service lawyer representing the government has found a serious discrepancy in his story. It turns out that Ochan was first interviewed five years ago, after sneaking in on a boat from Turkey and while living in a Newark homeless shelter. At the time, she points out, he submitted a written asylum request that mentioned nothing about his finger and in which he claimed to have escaped from the infamous Cobra Prison in Khartoum during a celebrated jailbreak. She submits this statement as Exhibit 7.

Ochan confers with his lawyer, who is upset because she is unaware of the earlier statement. He says that, over the course of five years, he forgot. Today, in any event, he admits that he has never been to Khartoum. He made that up, he says, because at his initial interview the immigration officials were openly hostile. They seemed not to have heard of the Sudan, and they asked if he was fleeing Communism, which has hardly been a factor there for two decades.

"I put in Khartoum because it is more famous than Juba," he explains. "I needed to impress them somehow." As for the finger, he says he didn't mention it in the written statement because he had already discussed it during the interview.

But the judge is concerned. Consistency is crucial in asylum hearings because of the frequent paucity of other evidence to support a claim of persecution. She had hoped to issue an oral decision from the bench today, she says, but "credibility is now such an obvious issue. Exhibit 7 has opened up a can of worms."

I have gotten to know Ochan in recent weeks, in particular at a demonstration he organized at the United Nations, on July 31, 1993, to publicize the persecution of Christians in the war on the Sudan, and I sympathize with him as we walk to the elevator.

"When will they give me back my life?" he asks. "I am like their prisoner."

At the same time, I doubt I will ever know him well. Asylum seekers, most of them so alone in the world and so at risk, have many secrets. I wonder with him, as I wondered with Dong, whether I appear as just another representative of The System, another person to impress. In his shoes, what would I do? All I can feel sure of is that he has gone through hell and would make a good neighbor. Unlike many of the millions who immigrate unofficially, he wants to be a part of the system; he craves legitimacy; he would cherish citizenship. The decision the judge will make, her balancing of sympathy and hardheadedness, will be in microcosm the decision that America and the rest of the developed world must make.

The Golden Rule in the
Age of the Global Village
Gerda Bikales

Gerda Bikales, a Holocaust survivor and immigrant, is currently president of E Pluribus Unum, a public interest group in Washington, D.C. "The Golden Rule in the Age of the Global Village" was originally published in *The Humanist* and appears here in revised form.

FOR THE LAST two decades, one of the most dynamic American growth industries has been the practice of immigration law. In the 1970s, some three hundred lawyers were specialists in immigration and affiliated with the immigration bar. By 1982, the American Immigration Lawyers Association had grown to 1,200 members. Ten years later, that number had tripled, to 3,600.

Not surprisingly, immigration admissions to the United States reflect a similar growth pattern. Between 1961 and 1970, 5.3 million immigrants were admitted; between 1971 and 1980, 7 million admissions were recorded; between 1981 and 1990, the number was 9.9 million. In 1992 alone, 1.9 million immigrants were admitted to permanent residence in our country—an all-time record.

The acceptance of more immigrants has not in any way diminished the backlog of people wanting to resettle in America. Our consulates across the world report larger numbers of applicants for immigration visas. Nearly three million people were waiting for visas in 1992, up from 2.2 million in 1988.

Refugee numbers worldwide have gone from 8 million in 1980 to 18 million in 1992. The majority of these desperate people are fervently hoping for a chance to rebuild their lives in our midst. America is the preferred destination for nearly all refugees.

Hundreds of thousands of people have chosen to bypass the legal obstacles to immigration altogether, entering and settling in the United States without the requisite documents. The Center for Immigration Studies estimates that by 1992 4.8 million people were living illegally in the country, and that this core population was expanding at the rate of about 300,000 every year.

The New Realities

Behind the crush for admission to the United States lie several developments of far-reaching consequence.

First, and most significant, is the continuing population explosion in all parts of the less developed world. Every year, more than 90 million people are added to the world's population, most of them in countries already incapable of supporting their population.

Overpopulation itself is an actual or potential cause of instability, creating masses of restless young people who face a lifetime of chronic underemployment. Furthermore, every political upheaval or natural disaster displaces more individuals than would have been the case if the area had been less populated. This causes rapid buildups of refugees, and the sheer number of unfortunate people in flight commands world attention.

Another major characteristic of our age is the presence of sophisticated electronic communications technology, which can quickly bring the suffering of the most remote and unfamiliar people, from every corner of the world, right into our living rooms. Night after night, the television image of the starving children of Somalia, victims of a total breakdown in civil government, became a silent guest at our plentiful dinner tables—a morally painful situation that eventually led to American military intervention on their behalf.

Finally, there is the fact that we have the ability to remove thousands of people from the locus of their misery and bring them to the United States. Only a relatively short plane flight separates the wretched refugees in the former Yugoslav republic of Bosnia from a safe and peaceful life in the United States.

These new realities—overpopulation, instant electronic news coverage, and mass transportation—raise serious questions about the adequacy of the traditional guidelines we call upon in trying to meet our moral obligations toward the world's less fortunate human beings.

The most fundamental principle of ethical behavior, as articulated by society's seats of moral authority, is invariably some version of the Golden Rule: Love thy neighbor as thyself. This precept is deeply ingrained in individuals raised in Judeo-Christian cultures. It underlies our standard codes of neighborliness. Appeals to it can produce collective acts of remarkable generosity. It can be said of Western societies, without exaggeration, that internalizing the Golden Rule is considered the true hallmark of a civilized human being.

It is obvious, though usually unstated in religious teachings, that there is a very practical side to the Golden Rule that strongly reinforces its moral sway. "Do unto others as you would have others do unto you" tacitly sets up a social contract that implies long-term mutual benefits: be helpful to your neighbor in his time of need, so that you can count on him to reciprocate when you, in turn, are helpless. The power of the Golden Rule lies precisely in the reinforcement of its lofty appeal to conscience by the practical wisdom of the command.

With the advent of modern instant communications, the neighborhood has been expanded well beyond the confines of one's community to include the whole world. The suffering of a hungry and hopeless Haitian becomes every bit as vivid as the tragedies that afflict the family next door. More so, perhaps. A sense of privacy separates us from our neighbor's pain, while the rawest emotions are unashamedly communicated on our television screens.

These demographic and technological changes pose a new challenge to the rule of the Golden Rule: how do I love my neighbor as myself, when *every* poor and downtrodden human being in this overpopulated world *is* my neighbor?

The Search for Moral Guidelines

The above question is very new. Until quite recently, moral decisions tended to be made on the basis of absolute principles that disregarded considerations of scale.

But in a world of limited resources, how many of the world's hundreds of millions of unfortunates is one to help? Is it better to share more fully with a few individuals or is less help to more people the better choice?

We have few guidelines to illuminate our path, as we earnestly grope for answers.

Traditionalist authorities might want to call upon the life of St. Francis of Assisi to support their views of moral obligation. This revered saint has given us an inspiring example of a man born to wealth who chose to abandon its comforts and to live a life of shared poverty as a mendicant among lepers and outcasts.

But renunciation is not a serviceable model for today's Americans. The appeal to our conscience is not for us to share the misery of the most miserable on this earth but to improve their lives through our acts of compassion and generosity. The number of totally selfless saints that a modern society can afford is rather small. A nation of good-hearted mendicants cannot long sustain itself, let alone help others.

The wise sharing of our possessions, rather than their renunciation, is the paradigm we seek. In this context, the example that comes to mind is that of St. Martin of Tours, who gave away one-half of his cloak to a naked beggar he encountered on the road. One wonders, however, what St. Martin would have done had he met up with twenty naked and shivering beggars. Would he have selected one or two for covering and let the others freeze? And, if so, on what basis would he have selected these fortunate few over all the others? Or would this holy man have split his garment into twenty-one equal but inadequate pieces, which would have shielded no one from the cold? Are both decisions equally virtuous, though one is patently foolish?

The Quantitative Aspects of Charity

For lack of better quantitative guidelines for charitable behavior, we can perhaps draw upon tithing as a nearly universal prescription. The concept that decent people should spend a tenth of their revenues on the Church and on good works is well-established throughout the Judeo-Christian world. A quota of 10 percent of income for charity is probably to be interpreted as a minimum, to be exceeded by those who can afford to give more. One respected source in the Jewish literature on *tzedakah* proposes a maximum of 20 percent, cautioning that those who give more run the risk of becoming paupers themselves.

A meaningful inhibition on excessive giving could be deduced from strong prohibitions in Jewish law against suicide. To knowingly risk serious injury to oneself and one's family, albeit in the interest of helping another, could be considered suicidal behavior, which is abhorrent.

In modern societies, many of the functions of the Church that were once financed by tithing have been taken over by governments. Through taxation, Americans already contribute far more than the traditional one-tenth to numerous social programs designed to help the sick, the elderly, the disabled, the very young, and the poor among us. Through taxation, they also contribute to numerous aid programs abroad, including significant payments to the United Nations for refugee relief programs.

In addition to "charity through taxation," Americans give privately to numerous good works, both here and in other countries. When disaster strikes anywhere, Americans can be counted on for generous assistance. Thus, through public and private channels, Americans are fulfilling the moral imperative of contributing at least one-tenth of their incomes to helping others.

Religious Authority in a Secular Society

Our country was founded by deeply devout people escaping persecution for their religious beliefs, and looking for a chance to worship freely on these shores. Despite these origins, America is a determinedly secular society. Religion has surely been a preeminent influence in our common culture, but it is by no means the only one. In fact, despite fairly high levels of church attendance, preoccupation with things spiritual is not one of our national characteristics. Unfriendly critics often describe us as materialistic. Friendlier observers might say that we are pragmatists, people who take pride in their good common sense. Science, and the technological changes it has spawned, have markedly shaped us and influenced the character of our people and our country.

In determining what immigration and refugee policies stand the test of compliance with the Golden Rule, the conclusions reached by religious leaders differ sharply from those reached by the vast majority of the American public. The difference lies, in part, in the classic dichotomy between faith and reason.

At issue is the question of how real, how immediate, and how tyrannical are our resource constraints. People of unshakable faith can afford to be rather less concerned about all this, convinced as they are that "God will provide." Resource management is definitely simpler for those who believe, literally or figuratively, the teaching that seven loaves of bread and a few fish can feed a multitude.

Most Americans, however, whether church-affiliated or not, rely on their empirical observations that quantities do matter. That is why they choose to have small families. That is why they want to reduce, rather than expand, the incessant flow of refugees and immigrants.

These differing understandings of the nature of resource constraints have produced a vocal coalition of religious leaders who unabashedly use their influence with politicians to plead for more refugee and immigrant admissions; on the other side we see much of the American public, experiencing severe job shortages, spiraling budget deficits, a declining standard of living, a sense of cultural unraveling, and suffering from a prolonged case of "compassion fatigue," resisting the official policy of increased immigration admissions.

Democratic societies can accommodate many divergent viewpoints, of course. It would hardly create a ripple of interest if those still anchored to the ethical standards of a time when "neighbor" meant the people next door would follow their own conscience and generously share whatever they have with the world's suffering poor. But immigrant and refugee admissions to the United States are not the religious leadership's to give. That gift must come from the American people, many of whom see a compelling need to cut back on immigration.

In our society, religious institutions and their leaders are highly respected and exert great moral influence. They have, however, been carefully kept from exercising official authority, in application of the principle of separation of Church and State. Yet, time and again, the religious leadership has skillfully manipulated its prestige and moral influence into political coercion, winning concessions on immigration, in a process somewhat akin to moral blackmail. The technique has been highly successful, but inevitably creates resentment.

Once the refugees are admitted to the United States, the costs of their resettlement and ongoing support do not fall crushingly upon the religious institutions that lobbied for their admission, but are imposed upon the American commonwealth. It is the taxpayer who is made to pick up the tab, and made to feel unworthy because he isn't happy about it.

Secular humanitarians have also found much to like in this arrangement. And so has that entire spectrum of professionals engaged in "the helping professions" and "human services," for whom the continued refugee influx represents not only a livelihood but a *raison d'être* and a source of social prestige.

The Permanent Crisis

Working together, the coalition of religious and secular humanitarian interests has succeeded in keeping American refugee and immigration policies on an expansionary course. It has failed, however, to alter the increasingly negative attitudes of many Americans toward massive immigration.

By any available measurement—national public opinion polls, constituent mail to congressional offices, offers from host families to sponsor incoming refugees—there has been a steady decline in support for more refugee resettlement in the United States.

There are many obvious explanations for this development, including fears about the economy and competition for jobs. But there are also some less obvious reasons:

1. *The failure to induce guilt.* In view of their historic generosity toward the world's poor and homeless, Americans fail to feel sinful because they are not doing more; on the

contrary, they tend to perceive pressure from the humanitarian lobby as a case of the self-righteous browbeating the righteous.

2. *The obligation toward America's disadvantaged.* In the 1960s Americans pledged themselves to helping our own disadvantaged minorities move toward full participation in American life. This has required enormous sacrifices on the part of the majority population, not only in unprecedented outlays of monies for social programs but also, through affirmative action and other compensatory programs, the sacrificing of opportunities for themselves and their children in the interest of greater social equality. Even so, the promise to disadvantaged Americans has not been fulfilled. Events such as the riots in Los Angeles in the spring of 1992 bespeak of increasing competition between inner-city blacks and immigrants, and point to immigration's role in obstructing the economic advancement of our black citizens.

3. *The breakdown in assimilation.* Two decades of massive immigration have strained our assimilative capacities. As immigration spiraled toward record levels, government policies veered away from encouraging assimilation, toward support for programs that emphasize cultural differences and downplay our common bonds. The consequences are palpable in our ethnically segregated classrooms and urban neighborhoods, and in the deterioration of intergroup relations. In many parts of the country, the evident displacement of English and of the core civic culture has alienated the members of the host society, who find themselves unwelcome and out of place in their own communities.

The issue of the cultural breakup of the American mainstream, and its relation to immigration, has not yet been fully articulated. But it is deeply felt by ever more Americans whose values and traditions are undergoing steady devaluation.

* * *

In the past, refugee "crises" seemed to be temporary problems that really could be resolved through swift resettlement in another country, particularly the United States. Under this assumption, we enacted legislation to accept some 400,000 displaced persons after World War II, and again 100,000 Hungarians after the failed revolt against Communism in 1956. The Cuban exodus that started when Castro came to power has brought us some one million refugees over two decades. The flow continues today at a diminished rate, but Castro's eventual demise is sure to launch another massive exodus. The Cuban migration should have given us pause to reflect on the chain effect of refugee admissions, but that phenomenon has hardly received any attention.

Beginning with the airlift of some 100,000 Indochinese in the wake of the American pullout from Vietnam in 1975, we have seen a steady succession of refugee crises from that part of the world. The first waves of refugees were accepted on the basis of their direct association with Americans during the war years, and the dangers they would face in the Communist takeover. In subsequent waves, the American connection with those in flight became more tenuous, and the term *refugee* underwent constant reinterpretation. Today, nearly a million Indochinese live in the United States, virtually all refugees who came after 1975 and their American-born children.

Other refugee crises have arisen across the globe with regularity—Afghans fleeing civil war, Ethiopians running from hunger and armed conflicts, Sri Lankans escaping religious and ethnic persecutions, Gypsies in flight from Romanian nationalists, Somalis running from starvation, Haitians running from poverty and oppression, and people running from the wars of vengeance wracking the former Soviet and Yugoslav republics.

These unceasing crises, projected in full color on our television screens, tend to have a dulling effect over time. This is not mean-spiritedness but a psychological defense mechanism that sets in after emotionally wrenching expenditures of sympathy. It is a fact of life that extraordinary mobilization of compassion cannot be maintained indefinitely; to stay psychologically and emotionally balanced, we must "turn off and tune out" at some point, in order to go on with the routine business of living our own lives.

It is especially difficult to adhere to the most generous interpretation of the Golden Rule when the "neighbor" is a stranger in a distant land. In the case of refugees from very different cultures in unfamiliar parts of the world, the assumption that we can expect reciprocity from these individuals in the future is very weak, and fails to reinforce the charitable impulse.

Yet Americans, like other people of goodwill, can become deeply aroused again and again when a new political or natural catastrophe is visited upon some corner of the world, and the distress is relayed through the electronic media. People's most generous impulses are reawakened, and once again they look to the traditional sources of moral authority for guidance.

The moral authorities they consult at those times have only predictable answers, from an era when the world was not yet a global village: "Open your door, open your heart, open your pocketbook."

Unfortunately, that is no longer serviceable advice. The symbolic resettlement of a small number of true political refugees is surely desirable and consistent with the benevolent affections of our people, but refugee resettlement in the United States has ceased to be a practical option. In an overpopulated world, the capacity to unleash disasters and to inflict suffering far exceeds this nation's capacity to absorb the victims.

The humanitarian establishment has been notably reticent to reexamine the meaning of neighborliness in the global village. It has been unwilling to acknowledge America's limits, and to assuage and comfort the troubled conscience of people seeking to do what's right.

The attitude of our moral leaders is not likely to change—

at least not as long as the government continues to pay for the resettlement work done by churches and other "humanitarian" lobbies, instead of requiring them to carry the costs of resettling the people they bring in.

We thus find ourselves in a moral leadership vacuum that must be filled. We can hope that a new generation of theologians and secular ethicists will soon arise, steeped in the ecological and demographic realities of the global village, to articulate an appropriate new Golden Rule.

But while we await a teaching tailored to our age, we may do well to ponder that of Rabbi Hillel, who, nearly a century before the Christian era, related selflessness to the imperatives of self-preservation, in a passage of disarming simplicity:

If *I* am not for myself, *who* will be for me?
If I am *only* for myself, what am I?
If not *now,* when?

Gender-Based Asylum
Julie Hessler

Julie Hessler's writing has appeared in the *Minneapolis Star Tribune, City Pages,* and *Iowa Woman.* "Gender-Based Asylum" was written for *Arguing Immigration.*

A REFUGEE IS currently defined by the United Nations as "a person who has a well-founded fear of persecution for reasons of race, religion, nationality, membership in a particular social group or political opinion." The UN's language is gender-neutral, but recently several countries, most notably Canada, have introduced the notion of gender into their definition of persecution. Their emphasis is on what it means to be persecuted as a woman.

It is a change that the United States, which, like most countries, has no specific policies regarding gender-based persecution, would be wise to consider.

In 1991, when Nada (a pseudonym), a Saudi Arabian woman, filed in Canada for refugee status on the grounds of gender persecution, her application was denied. Canadian officials rejected her argument that her refusal to wear a veil and her public opposition to Saudi Arabia's oppressive laws against women placed her life in danger if she returned home. But after public protests on Nada's behalf, Canada's immigration minister overruled the refugee-hearing panel. He granted Nada admission to Canada for humanitarian reasons.

As a result of Nada's case, the Canadian Immigration and

Refugee Board drafted guidelines for dealing with future claims of gender-based persecution in a twenty-page document on "persecution as applied to women seeking admission to Canada as refugees." Although the guidelines are not legally binding, when a refugee claims gender persecution, Canadian immigration officials must now consider "whether in the petitioner's home country 'state authorities inflict, condone or tolerate violence, including sexual or domestic violence.' " Nada was never granted refugee status, but since the guidelines were implemented, that status has been granted to several other women claiming gender-based persecution.

United States courts, working without any comparable guidelines, continue to apply the UN's definition of refugee to all persons—male or female—seeking asylum in the United States. Women seeking refugee status must prove a fear of persecution based on one of the five grounds for asylum. U.S. courts, for example, granted asylum to several Chinese refugees—both women and men—who fled that country's one-child-per-family and forced-sterilization policies. A judge declared that opposition to such policies "constitutes political opinion."

But U.S. officials continue to act as if adding gender as a sixth ground for asylum would confound traditional notions of what kinds of acts constitute persecution. Consider, for example, the case of Sofia Campos-Guardado, a native of El Salvador. The transcript of her case reads as follows: "Forcing the women to watch, they hacked the flesh from the men's bodies with machetes, finally shooting them to death. The male attackers then raped the women, including Ms. Campos-Guardado, while the woman who accompanied the attackers shouted political slogans. The assailants cut the victims loose, threatening to kill them unless they fled immediately. They ran and were taken to a hospital in El Salvador."

Sofia Campos-Guardado's request for asylum was denied by the 5th Circuit U.S. Court of Appeals in 1987. Despite her brutalization, the court concluded that she "had not shown that the attackers harmed her in order to overcome any of *her own* political opinions." Her rape, which occurred at her uncle's farm, was instead viewed as a consequence of his involvement in a land-reform movement. As Deborah Sontag wrote in the *New York Times,* the fact that an assailant had since threatened to kill Campos-Guardado and her family if she were to reveal him was deemed "entirely personal." The court concluded that Campos-Guardado "failed to show that the harm she fears—no matter how likely—is on account of 'political opinion' or 'membership in a social group,' as those terms are used in the statute."

• • •

Gender provides a context for a series of acts that were, in the past, considered personal, private, random, and female, rather than political, public, systematic, and male. Under Canada's guidelines, Campos-Guardado would in all likelihood have been granted refugee status under the guideline that specifically addresses cases in which women fear persecution based on kinship.

What explains the reluctance of the United States and other countries to adopt gender as a sixth ground for asylum? Perhaps the sheer number of refugees they might have to consider. As many as twenty thousand Muslim women and girls may have been raped since the war in Bosnia-Herzegovina began. Worldwide eighty million women are said to have been victims of clitoridectomies. According to a report in *Ms.* magazine, in one week eight hundred women were arrested in Tehran for dress-code violations.

Clearly, the United States cannot address every case of gender-based oppression. But the extent of the problem should not prevent us from setting priorities and taking action regarding legitimate claims of gender-based persecution.

The dangers women face may be different from the dangers men face, but their fears are well-founded. A rape, a forced marriage, a forced abortion are as threatening to life as the fear of Communism or religious persecution that has allowed so many refugees asylum in America. The time has come to acknowledge as much.

Right now the United States can learn from Canada's efforts to change its gender-blind refugee policy. But we can also do Canada one better. An intelligent and effective United States policy on gender-based persecution will require a systemic, two-tier approach. The first tier must be legal and consist of binding guidelines that make gender persecution a legitimate ground for asylum. The second tier must be more subjective—more female, as it were. It must acknowledge the widespread nature of gender persecution and insist on good-faith efforts—in foreign policy as well as international law—that go beyond asylum in providing relief for women.

Law and Asylum
Viet D. Dinh

Viet D. Dinh recently completed a clerkship for Judge Laurence H. Silberman, U.S. Court of Appeals, D.C. Circuit. His writing has appeared in the *New York Times, Harvard Law Review,* and *Reconstruction.* "Law and Asylum" was written for *Arguing Immigration.*

"**WHITEHEAD BOAT PEOPLE** Detention Center, Hong Kong." A hand-painted sign marks the towering fence—three rows of barbed wire topped with coils of gleaming razor edges—that separates me from my oldest sister. Outside, I am free and protected by the blue covers of an American passport. Locked inside for nearly three years, Van and her children share the camp with thousands of other refugees, all hoping they will not be forced back to the repressive Vietnam they thought they had escaped.

I last saw Van fourteen years earlier, when I escaped from Vietnam in 1978. My father, an official in the former government, was being held in a reeducation camp. To avoid retribution for our family's departure, he had to escape the camp when we left. My mother was to lead the children out of the country. That left Van remaining to execute my father's escape and help him live on the run. She bribed the camp guards so my father could jump the fence, then drove a motorcycle that carried him to a hiding place three hours away.

When we arrived in Malaysia after twelve days at sea, a patrol boat fired at us—forcing our vessel, crippled by a storm, back to the open waters. Without adequate supplies, we turned back after dark and sank our boat near shore. The next morning, United Nations officials admitted us into a refugee camp, ignoring our accounts of the gunboat assault. After immigration interviews, we were admitted to America. Van sprang my father from the camp and helped him, after twenty-five unsuccessful attempts, to escape Vietnam and join our family in 1983.

Van fled herself in 1989 and encountered an even ruder welcome when she arrived in Hong Kong. Up to the late 1980s Vietnamese refugees, for the most part, enjoyed the solicitude of the Western world. Those who arrived in refugee camps in Malaysia, Thailand, and Hong Kong were quickly resettled in Canada, Australia, or America. But the compassion waned, and resettlement of refugees in Western nations failed to keep pace with their arrival. Faced with the bottleneck, Hong Kong reversed its policy of automatically granting asylum to all Vietnamese. Those who arrived after June 1988 were subject to a screening interview. If officials thought they were not political refugees, they were forced back to Vietnam. International outcry against the policy prompted Hong Kong to stop repatriating refugees forcibly; instead, the refugees were locked indefinitely in detention camps to wear down their resolve and make them "volunteer" to return to Vietnam. So Van arrived in Hong Kong with dreams of freedom but went through three years of detention on a desolate island.

Our family is now reunited. Hong Kong immigration officials finally gave Van a screening interview. She told of the harassment that was a way of life for politically suspect families and proved her eligibility for asylum. Van arrived in Portland, Oregon, in September 1992. The unhappy parallels to her story are, however, plenty. Other Vietnamese refugees wait longer for an interview; 85 percent of them are denied asylum and forced back to the country from which they fled.

And thousands of Haitians cannot even tell their story.

The U.S. Coast Guard stops them before they reach our border and formally apply for asylum. They are returned to Haiti, even though, as one federal court found, "hundreds of Haitians have been killed, tortured, detained without a warrant, or subjected to violence and the destruction of their property because of their political beliefs." What was for me an isolated incident of cruelty is now an international policy: let them drift, let them die, but don't let them land on our soil.

• • • •

On June 21, 1993, the Supreme Court decided *Sale* v. *Haitian Centers Council,* quelling the last hope for Haitian asylum seekers. The steps that led to *Sale* go back much further in time, however. In 1981 President Reagan proclaimed that Haitian entry into south Florida was "a serious national problem." He ordered the Coast Guard to intercept Haitian boats on the high seas and to repatriate the passengers if they do not, in an on-board interview, establish a credible claim to asylum. In October 1991, an unprecedented number of Haitians fled after the ouster of Jean Aristide, overwhelming the interdiction and screening program. President Bush responded by ordering that captured Haitians be returned without interviews, even though a record number were being "screened in" after the preliminary interview. Upon assuming office, President Clinton reversed his campaign promise of guaranteed screenings and continued to enforce President Bush's interdiction and summary repatriation policy. In *Sale,* the Court held that interdicted Haitians can find no relief from the actions of the President in federal court.

The decision of all three Presidents to stop the Haitians before they reach U.S. borders is understandable. Immigration law divides aliens into three distinct groups for enormously different treatment. Those who have been admitted, or somehow make their way, into the country can be expelled only after a deportation hearing and enjoy a panoply of procedural protections, including certain due-process rights under the Constitution. Those who present themselves at the border but have not been admitted are entitled to an "exclusion" procedure provided by statute, including appeals that can occupy several years. Finally, as the Court stated in *Sale,* those who have not made it to the border have no statutory or constitutional rights. By repelling asylum seekers before they arrive at the borders, the President prevents them from being entitled to "exclusion" interview and appeal procedures that threaten to overwhelm an already burdened system.

This three-tiered framework of rights began with the journey of a young Chinese laborer, Chae Chan Ping. He entered the United States in 1875 under the Burlingame Treaty, which guaranteed free immigration from China in order to import cheap labor. The treaty was modified, and in 1882 Congress responded to nativist sentiments by suspending Chinese immigration for a decade. Chinese who had entered before 1880, however, were permitted to stay and to reenter the country if they secured a certificate prior to departure. Chae Chan Ping obtained a certificate and left. While he was in China, Congress again changed the law to bar all Chinese—even those with reentry certificates.

Trapped on his return ship, the *Belgic,* Chae Chan Ping sued and argued that Congress could not withdraw his right to reenter, an action that he thought violated the Constitution. In 1889 the Supreme Court disagreed, setting forth the basic framework of American immigration law. Finding that the power to exclude aliens "is an incident of every independent nation," the Court held that Congress's decision on the exclusion of immigrants "is conclusive upon the judiciary"—the alien has no constitutional rights. In a later case, the Court stated this plenary legislative power in its purest form: "[O]ver no conceivable subject is the legislative power of Congress more complete than it is over [the exclusion of aliens]."

Chae Chan Ping had not physically entered the United States, held as he was in San Francisco Bay while his lawyers worked. Kaoru Yamataya, by contrast, had been in Seattle for four days when she was arrested for deportation, after an immigration inspector determined that she—a pauper—could not legally stay. The Court ruled on her situation in 1903. While not stopping Yamataya from being deported, it stated that an immigrant who had entered the United States stood on different footing from one seeking admission. Due process of law does not permit such a person "to be taken into custody and deported without giving all opportunity to be heard upon the questions involving his right to be and remain in the United States."

The two cases thus explicate the "entry doctrine" in immigration law: a person who has entered the country is entitled to some due-process protection while an alien who is at the border has no rights other than those afforded by Congress and the President. In the words of the Supreme Court, "Whatever the procedure authorized by Congress is, it is due process as far as an alien denied entry is concerned."

Up until 1980, this distinction between exclusion and deportation was crucial in asylum claims, since the mandate of the Immigration and Nationality Act that an immigrant not be returned to a country if his "life or freedom would be threatened in such country on account of race, religion, nationality, membership in a particular social group, or political opinion" applied only to deportation of immigrants already in the country, not to exclusion of aliens seeking entry. Congress changed the law in 1980 and extended the protection to excludable aliens—thereby erasing perhaps the cruelest distinction predicated upon the entry doctrine.

But in 1993 the Court in *Sale* found a new distinction, that between aliens who have presented themselves at the border and those who, for whatever reason, did not make it there. Arguing that "[w]hen it desires to do so, Congress knows how to place the high seas within the jurisdictional reach of a statute," the Court held that the 1980 act does not speak to the status of aliens captured outside U.S. borders—pregnantly noting that "[t]he wisdom of the policy choices made by Presidents Reagan, Bush, and Clinton is not a matter for our consideration."

• • •

The question we now face is whether the policy should stand. Should we condone the discrimination between migrants who reach our border and those whom we are able to intercept on the high seas? I think not. Asylum is too important—both to those who seek it and to our tradition as a sanctuary to the persecuted—to be predicated on such legalistic hair-splitting.

I recognize that a nation must be able to exclude aliens in order to establish its sovereignty. It is only through defining the terms of membership that a community maintains a political and cultural identity independent from others. Self-preservation permits us to exclude those whom we regard as a threat to our community and those whom we think are unworthy of admission. And because we want to preserve our democratic institutions, we can justly demand that aliens whom we admit conform with our standards of self-governance and integrate into our political culture.

But because the power to exclude derives from the need to lay the foundations of our community, the standards that we employ to exclude aliens have to reflect the values of our society; our immigration policies must be consonant with our democratic ideals. At the core of these ideals is an assumption of equality for all. Our immigration policies therefore must embody neutral standards that are applied consistently to all those who seek admission, absent a logical and justifiable basis for differentiation.

No such logical distinction exists to justify the disparate treatment we currently accord to asylum seekers who reach our shores and those whom we intercept on the high seas.

Supporters of our present asylum policy point to the fact that permitting the intercepted aliens to reach our shores would entitle them to extensive statutory rights. The formal exclusion procedures could occupy several years, while the aliens are detained in Florida camps or paroled into the country temporarily; permitting all asylum seekers to reach our shores would in turn cause administrative nightmares and unwanted immigration (even if temporary). But these concerns are arguments in favor of reforming our exclusion procedures, not of precluding wholesale consideration of a class of asylum claims. A consistent policy would afford *all* who seek asylum an opportunity to tell their story, even if inadequate resources required that opportunity to be more limited than present exclusion procedures.

Indeed, any distinction between asylum seekers at our borders and those on the high seas is artificially created by our intervening actions; by intercepting boats in international waters, we corral the asylum seekers into a particular status group for disparate treatment. We have pledged not to turn our backs on anyone who has a well-founded fear of persecution, and whether or not we honor that covenant should not depend on whether our Coast Guard successfully repels those who seek our mercy before they can ask for it.

To maintain a democratically consistent asylum policy would, I recognize, not be easy. The administrative demands would require a larger immigration bureaucracy than we now have. And reform to streamline exclusion procedures faces imposing obstacles. Asylum reform could also result in a flood of refugees who would add to our welfare rolls and lengthen our unemployment lines. But if we believe these obstacles are insurmountable, we must be willing to say that although we would like to give refuge to all who are persecuted, we cannot do so given our limited capacity for mercy. In any case, whatever our capacity for asylum, we owe all claimants at least an equal opportunity to present their case.

We cannot rely on legal gimmicks to escape the burdens a genuinely democratic and morally consistent asylum policy would place upon us.

President Clinton himself acknowledged this problem when, on May 8, 1994, he again changed course and announced limited screenings, on coast guard ships, for Haitians. It was the moral thing to do, a step in the right direction that was prodded by the twenty-seven-day protest fast of Randall Robinson, the executive director of the TransAfrica Foundation. Pity that the president's decision seemed less a recognition of democratic obliglation than a foreign policy dictated by a hunger strike.

When Hong Kong finally gave my sister a screening interview, Van talked about the persecution she suffered in Communist Vietnam. She told of the time when the police took my father away to the reeducation camp and of the harassment she endured when they discovered her aid to my fugitive father. It was a simple story, taking her about an hour to tell and the interviewer another hour to verify. They are two hours for which she risked everything and that gave her freedom. They are also two hours that all asylum seekers should have, whether or not we admit them.

Acknowledgments

I have benefited once again from the research of Bob Struckman and Dina Pancoast. Brian Morton and Sean Wilentz did the kind of close readings that amount to giving blood.